JESUS OVER BLACK

HOW MY FAITH TRANSFORMED ME INTO A CONSERVATIVE WITHIN THE BLACK COMMUNITY

PHILIP BLACKETT

To my grandmother, Josephine Gaines Wade, who was to me as Lois was to Timothy in the Bible (2 Timothy 1:5) and passed down to me the greatest legacy anyone can pass to the next generation: knowledge of God and His Word towards establishing and building a lifelong relationship with Jesus Christ as Lord and Savior.

You inspired me to do the same and stand strong for Jesus and pass down this legacy from you to my children, my grandchildren and future generations. Thank you for finding me worthwhile to invest in and to bring into God's Kingdom. I will forever love you and be eternally grateful for God blessing me with you in my life.

***

To my own personal heroes of the faith: Dr. Tony Evans, Dr. Albert Mohler, Rev. Billy Graham, Bishop T.D. Jakes, Dr. Voddie Baucham, Bishop Gilbert E. Patterson, Dr. Myron Golden, Pastor Adrian Rogers, and Tim Tebow.

You men stand for Christ within a fallen world and instructed, challenged, and mentored me from afar in how not to be an Undercover Christian or Secret Agent Saint but to boldly witness to others of who God is, what He has done, and what He will do for His people and His Kingdom now, in the near future, and in eternity.

Thank you for empowering me to speak up for Jesus and to share His Good News to the world for both evangelism and discipleship.

PREFACE

"In matters of style, swim with the current; in matters of principle, stand like a rock." — Thomas Jefferson

In the fabric of our society, threads of spirituality and politics intertwine, often becoming indistinguishable. Yet, as a vessel of faith and conviction, we must navigate this interwoven landscape with discernment and courage. This journey is one I know intimately, one that has compelled me to pen the narrative you hold in your hands—a guide for those who stand at the crossroads of faith and cultural expectation, seeking direction that does not compromise their core beliefs.

Rooted deeply in the Christian tradition and informed by a life of diverse professional experiences, this book is my invitation to you—to explore and affirm a conservative stance within the context of the Black Christian experience. Its pages bid you to discover a spiritual and political harmony that resonates with your deepest convictions.

Throughout my life, I have encountered many who, like you, yearn for a compelling voice to articulate the nuances of their journey. Individuals seeking to reconcile the vibrancy of their faith with the hue of their political views have shared their stories with me. Through kitchen-table conversations and quiet moments of reflection, I've seen the struggle to align spiritual truths with a conservative worldview, often in a space that expects a different course.

These stories, your stories, lit the pathway that led to this work. They are the living testament to the necessity of bridging spiritual truth and personal ideology without yielding to the societal pressures that urge conformity.

My pilgrimage through the corridors of Wall Street and Corporate America, the stewardship of owning a seven-figure business, and the spiritual quest that culminated in a Masters of Divinity degree have indelibly shaped my perspective. Each step has reinforced my belief in the transformative power of faith and the disciplined pursuit of entrepreneurial success. This book draws from those wellsprings, offering actionable insights designed to edify and equip you on your journey.

From the classrooms of Harvard to the spiritual halls of The Southern Baptist Theological Seminary, I have been blessed to sit under the tutelage of great minds. Their wisdom fills these pages, along with the love and support of my wife Mayra, my twins Sofia and Elizabeth, and my brethren in Alpha Phi Alpha. To these pillars of strength, I extend my deepest appreciation.

I am humbled that you have chosen to invest your time with me. It is not a trust I take lightly. This narrative is for those of you who walk in the light of Christ and yet find the cultural labels restrictive, who reject the notion that one's race dictates one's political affiliation or overall identity. There are no prerequisites for this journey, only an open heart and a quest for truth.

In a resonant and guiding voice, I invite you to delve into these pages. Here, find the solace and strength to claim an identity anchored firmly in faith and conservative values. Thank you for entrusting me with a portion of your story. May the journey ahead bring clarity, conviction, and the courage to stand resolute in your beliefs as we navigate the waterways of conservatism in the Black Christian journey.

CONTENTS

INTRODUCTION

*"Now when Joshua was near Jericho, he looked up and saw
a man standing in front of him with a drawn sword in his
hand. Joshua went up to him and asked, "Are you for us or for
our enemies?" "Neither," he replied, "but as commander of the
army of the LORD I have now come." Then Joshua fell facedown
to the ground in reverence, and asked him, "What message does
my Lord have for his servant?" – Joshua 5:13-14 (NIV)*

***

**For a period of time growing up, I was raised believing that
being black or African American was the most important part
of my identity.** I was raised in the South, a generation removed from
the Civil Rights Movement, and at the time of my childhood, there
was still much inequality, prejudice and racism that was seemingly
and disproportionately impacting African Americans vs. other groups
of people. However, while such struggles for freedom and equality

may serve as a "trauma bond" with other people with darker skin complexions and a shared American history with myself, I grew up later realizing that there was a much greater history to me than being shipped to the New World as slaves in the 17th century or roaming across the African continent as historical kings and queens of great tribes.

I realized that my history started with the first man created on Earth: Adam. Adam was where all humans of every color, ethnicity, tribe and creed came from. God created Adam, which makes God my creator too. When Adam and Eve sinned by eating the forbidden fruit after Satan's temptation, all humankind – regardless of our differences on the outside – shared a common inheritance in original sin. Such sin would color the way we see each other, as well as God. **Such sin would lead to us believing that one group of people is more worthy or valuable than another because of one's lighter (or darker) color of skin.** The sin of racism has a father and that is the original sin of disobedience against God's command and putting our faith and trust in a god other than the one true God, our shared Heavenly Father and the original creator of all that life is and was designed to be on Earth. Our future as a broken people is doomed because of sin, where our future ultimately leads to death and the grave, eternally separated from God.

But God had other plans and embarked on a rescue mission, despite numerous human failures throughout the Old Testament to redeem and save God's people, where God would send His Son, the second and last Adam, in Jesus Christ to come down from Heaven to Earth and expose us to a new way of living through divine revelation, while walking among us humans. **Jesus would later die in our place on an old, rugged cross for our sins** – serving as the spotless lamb whose blood previously saved the Israelites from divine judgment from God in Egypt back in the Book of Exodus – **and ultimately provided the way towards reconciliation in a renewed relationship not only with God but also with each other as His people with a shared history, lineage, and mission as part of God's Kingdom**.

The Bible, in its entirety, is clear on where Christians stand in identity with the image of God bearing within us as followers of Jesus Christ. **Billions of people throughout the world today, as I write this, make a choice on how they identify themselves and what is the most important contributor of what makes them who they are.** Some people choose to base their identity on the color of their skin, the type of person they love, the sports team they cheer for, the political party they follow, or numerous other indicators. **As for me, my identity is based on following Jesus Christ as my Lord and Savior.** That supersedes my race, ethnic history, nationality, sexuality, or any other aspect about me, for all such aspects are submitted to what is most important to me: to serve God as a good and faithful steward of all that He has entrusted to me during my limited time here on Earth to follow after Jesus as one of His disciples to bring God's heavenly kingdom to Earth, as well as to bring the spiritually lost back to God's family.

I recognize that my candid thoughts within this book may be controversial for some readers, and I also recognize that that is OK. **I hope for this book to serve as a way to help bring an honest marketplace of ideas for people to debate the merits of each idea with one another respectfully, rather than resort to immature and juvenile name-calling, character-shaming, and overall avoidance of any fruitful conversation, dialogue, and understanding of one another's viewpoints and worldviews in order to arrive at a better decision on how one will respond in how one believes to**

live his or her life afterwards. I understand that my saying this will not necessarily prevent people to call me outside of my name, even if it comes from reputable TV networks and talk show hosts potentially or anonymous social media trolls. I may even lose so-called friends and acquaintances who may not want to associate with someone who is honest with his thoughts and feelings, thus putting into question whether someone is truly inclusive of a "diversity of thought", rather than diversity and inclusion of one's race, gender, sexual orientation, and religion. **If we truly want to be a people embracing of diversity, we must recognize that diversity goes beyond skin deep, and it includes the diversity of ideas, beliefs, and worldviews for us to consider thoughtfully and choose whether to lovingly agree or respectfully disagree with.**

The other motivation for writing this book is the thought that there are more African Americans like me who share a similar Biblical worldview and identity as followers of Jesus Christ globally. Especially in America, there seems to be growing antagonism against Christians, especially from one side of the political spectrum. To believe that the Bible is true and without error carries an air amongst some liberals as being conservative. **News flash: the evangelical population is not entirely filled with white people, and if the Democratic Party, for example, wants to typecast black people as all thinking and believing the same, regardless of how far extreme the political party may go left and away from traditional, Biblical values, the party may be in for a rude awakening as there can be a growing exodus of African Americans, including myself, that are seen as conservative based on what we believe and may find the Republican party closer to home.** Don't get it twisted though: we may not agree with everything that the Republican Party espouses, and **I consider myself a Republican-light Christian.** However, I can say that while Jesus Christ remains first in my commitment as my Lord and Savior, which means that Jesus also is above politics, I also can acknowledge that I am much more likely to vote Republican than I am to vote Democrat as evident over the past five presidential elections since I was able to start voting in college.

At the same time, **I recognize that I, among other similar African Americans, may be living at a crossroads here. We may get flack from all sides for what we believe. As a Christian, we may get denigrated by people on the far Left for being traditional, conservative or old-fashioned. On the right side, we may wonder if we may truly be accepted by Republicans or Libertarians, even though the majority of them do not look like us. Among other black people that we may disagree with on certain issues or viewpoints, we may be called Uncle Toms or be denied of our blackness, simply because of a different point of view. Overall, we may struggle to find a consistent home altogether. However, that is why I rest in focusing my efforts on being aligned with God's family first over everything else.** I know that the Bible says that, in the end, every knee will bow and every tongue will ultimately confess that Jesus is Lord. In the book of Revelation, the Bible speaks of God's people consisting of every nation, tribe, and language in a truly envisioned multi-cultural, multi-ethnic, multi-racial family united in Christ. **That unity is what is most important to me, since I believe that what God intended originally will come to pass in the end.** In that case, I might as well live that way in preparation to that great day into eternity with Him. This is why I am writing this book, not only to share my worldview with you, but also to expose you to potentially a different way to view living life in anticipation of what God has planned for us, **in hopes**

of helping you make the right response towards choosing Jesus over any other form of identity for yourself.

My Personal Journey of Faith

I grew up in Memphis, TN in a single-parent household with my little sister in the South. We were supported by my aunt and grandparents, who all attended the same family church of my grandparents. It was a Baptist church. It was where I was baptized as a young boy. I went to Sunday School in the mornings before church service, as well as Vacation Bible School during the summertime. My grandmother and grandfather were very active in the church, often serving as great examples of service within the church ministry. **I got my Christian roots from my grandparents, especially my grandmother**. I remember her Bible used to be near the nightstand and living room table by the telephone. She was the one that first instilled in me the importance of having a lifelong relationship with the Lord. That legacy would carry with me throughout my life to today.

As I got older, I went to different churches from different congregations ranging from African Methodist Episcopal to Disciples of Christ. The pastors had different preaching styles, yet they came pretty accurately close to the stereotype of a Southern black preacher. Before high school, I attended a school with a significant Jewish population, where my social life on the weekends at one point were attending bar mitzvahs and bat mitzvahs when the Titanic movie premiered. I remember when I took an introduction to philosophy and ethics class in high school that I didn't pay much attention to such philosophers as Aristotle, Plato, Kant, and Descartes if their philosophy differed from what Jesus said and what was written in the Bible. When I left for college, I took my Life Application Study Bible with me. I still have it to this day and read from it regularly. Why? In the margins of the pages, there were notes and commentary to help me make sense of the Bible verses that I was reading. There were maps showing the locations of where the stories took place, as well as character profiles for me to study. In the back was an one-year reading plan that helped me read through the whole Bible from Genesis to Revelation. All of these contributed to me keeping with my Bible in my dorm room, taking it to church on Sundays, and referencing it when I went through dilemmas and temptations in college as a young adult. I was walking with God, but I was also trying to fit in with my social circle in college as one of the popular guys in class and with a steady girlfriend, or at least an active love life.

God and I got real close around 2008 and 2009 during the Great Recession. At the time, there was a huge economic slowdown. I got laid off from my job on Wall Street, and I was trying to figure out how to put the pieces back together in my life quickly after such a disappointing job loss. There were moments that I was alone in my place, where the enemy was definitely tempting me to give up on life or to do something that would self-sabotage the trajectory of my life, while battling loneliness and depression. **Jesus was with me during those rough times. It was the Word of God that encouraged me to keep going. For the next 15 years or so, going through life's ups and downs, the one thing that was consistent in my life, especially after my grandparents passed away, was God. If it was not for God, I would not be here with you today. Given all that He has done for me throughout my life, how can I possibly serve anyone else outside of God? He has brought me through too much for me to consider turning my back on Him to go after a false god or cultural idol.**

After business school, I married my wife and we had twin daughters during our first year of marriage. Guess who specifically prayed for twin daughters? Yep. Me. Given the odds of giving birth to twin daughters, I know that my daughters are an answered prayer from God every time I look into their eyes many years later. One week, while the girls were really little, we took our first family trip out of town to Charlotte, NC. North Carolina always has a special place in my heart, since that was where I went for college. We were going to Charlotte for a work trip for my wife, who was attending a convention. **Of all the things that I wanted to experience while our family was down in Charlotte, one thing reigned supreme in my mind. I wanted to visit the Billy Graham Museum at his home.** Beforehand, I had watched a few of his evangelistic sermons on television, and God spoke to me through those sermons. **I was already a Christian, yet I felt God using the late Rev. Billy Graham and his life as an example for me to inquire how can I be more of service to God.** Going through the many exhibits and learning more about Billy's life, how he came to faith, and all that he and his family endured and struggled with in order for God to use him to spread the Gospel around the world, all of it was very inspiring for me. I left there asking God how He could use me in a similar way as He did for Billy Graham. Writing this book has been a clue of where God wants to take me for my good and for His glory.

In 2023, after graduating from seminary with my Masters of Divinity degree, God prompted me in my heart to take the next step to serve Him. He stirred in me the nerve to not only start preaching His Word online on a weekly basis. He also led me to take my thoughts and put them on paper in this book that you are reading. Why? **Because many of the people that I looked up to growing up who preached from the pulpit are either getting older, retiring, or have already** passed away. **Where will the next generation of preachers, evangelists and disciple makers come from?** Especially in our world today that is becoming more and more antagonistic towards God and His Word and His people. **While I was looking for someone else to step up and represent Christ boldly and publicly, God pointed the mirror back at me, reminding me of Isaiah 6:8:** *"Then I heard the voice of the Lord saying, 'Whom shall I send? And who will go for us?' And I said, 'Here am I. Send me!"* Send me Lord. Though I may be afraid of what happens afterwards, send me Lord. You have been too good for me and my family. I trust you and love you and want to be a good and faithful steward in fulfilling your mission to bring more of your Heavenly Kingdom here on Earth. I am also inspired to step up for my young family at home. **As the secular culture surrounds us in our schools, smartphones, social media, televisions, music, and news with things in opposition to God and what He shares in the Bible, I must take a stand for Jesus and for other Christians as an example to live out Joshua 24:15 in saying** *"as for me and my household, we will serve the Lord."* That is what has me writing this book to you now. **It's time for us as Christians to make Jesus the Lord over our lives, as well as our Savior. It is time for us to live on purpose, united in Christ, choosing to be identified more with Jesus than anything else**.

Following Jesus over Everything Else

Now, what do I mean by "Jesus over Black"? **To be clear, "Jesus over Black" means that the first and most important thing that identifies me is not the fact that I am a black man or an African American**. Yes, that is important. God made me black as part of His creation. I don't deny that or try to ignore color here. However, **being**

a Christian is more significant to my identity as a follower of Jesus Christ. Being black did not save me from my sin. Jesus did. In fact, we live in a world that I could receive proportionally more trouble than others because of my black skin, depending on where in the United States I am located and the time of day and the situation at hand. In any case, Jesus has been with me through the good and bad times, when things were going well or when I found myself in trouble. Following Jesus to be more like Him each and every day, while also doing my part to help bring others back within God's family through repentance of their sins, reconciliation with God, and belief in Jesus Christ as Lord and Savior – this is what drives me each day for the rest of my life. It is such a part of me that it has become a primary part of my identity.

Jesus is more important than any other potential replacement of Him as our identity. More important than our race, our gender, our sexuality, our job, our possessions, our wealth, our political party, our ideology. **Jesus is more important than everything else. That is why, as Christians, we should put Jesus in His proper place as our Lord and Savior: Jesus over everything else. Jesus over Black. Jesus over Hispanic. Jesus over my manhood. Jesus over feminism. Jesus over America. Jesus over your country of origin. Jesus over Democratic Party. Jesus over Republican Party. Jesus over Libertarian Party. Jesus reigns over everything, for God does not take second place, because He only deserves to be first.** This is why Jesus is over my blackness, which can be considered as conservative within not only the black community, but also the worldly culture at large.

If you ask, "What does it mean to be conservative in today's society?", one way to view it is your belief in the Bible as the Word of God. **If you believe that the Bible is inerrant, infallible, and worthy**

of serving as the objective standard of truth in how we live in relation to God and with one another, congratulations! You will more than likely be seen as conservative in our world today. If you believe that what God says is right in His Word is right and what He says is wrong (sin) in His Word is wrong, congratulations! Our culture, particularly of the Western world, would deem you conservative compared to what it believes. If you agree with the Word of God that God rules with BOTH justice and righteousness, and not just justice or how the world defines as "justice", congratulations! Once again, you, my friend, would be seen as conservative in the world we live in today. The question though is: alongside myself, along these lines, who else is conservative with me? The answer may surprise you, for the world of Bible-believing evangelicals is much broader than the all-white conservatives who love a particular political candidate that much of the broader media would like you to believe, especially within the United States.

Jesus' Two Greatest Commandments

When you pick up the Bible, it can be pretty intimidating for a number of reasons. One, the Bible is so big with so many pages, chapters and verses. The more important reason why it can be seen as intimidating is that you should view it for what it is: the Word of God. All of the Scripture is God-breathed, where the authors of each book was divinely inspired on what to write, so that it was not solely what the human authors wanted to write but more so, what God intended to reveal to us through His Word. For many of us, we want to simplify the Bible to something chewable, even at the risk of not understanding the whole story, the full context, and the entire narrative of how God created the world, we humans messed it up with sin, and God sent

His Son from heaven to earth to redeem us, so that we can have the opportunity to choose to turn away from our sins in repentance and to choose Jesus as our Lord and Savior in a reconciled relationship with God and His family both now and in eternity.

However, for the sake of this book, to help illustrate how my Christian faith has transformed me into a conservative within the Black community as applied to the world today, I want to focus on the two greatest commandments that Jesus shared with His people during His ministry. Yes, there were ten commandments delivered by Moses in the Old Testament, and those commandments still apply today, despite many who desire to write off the Old Testament and to focus simply on the New Testament, especially the red letters that Jesus spoke. While I embrace the entire Bible as the truth and as the cornerstone of my perspective in how I view the world around me, I want to focus on how these two commandments apply to some of the most pertinent issues of our age today.

And the Bible says in Matthew 22:34-40, *"Hearing that Jesus had silenced the Sadducees, the Pharisees got together. One of them, an expert in the law, tested him with this question: 'Teacher, which is the greatest commandment in the Law?'* **Jesus replied: 'Love the Lord your God with all your heart and with all your soul and with all your mind. This is the first and greatest commandment. And the second is like it: 'Love your neighbor as yourself.' All the Law and the Prophets hang on these two commandments.'"**

Love God. Love your neighbor as yourself. Jesus says that all the Law (dating back to Moses and the 10 commandments) and the Prophets (of the Old Testament) hang on these two commandments, meaning that we can adhere to the Law and the Prophets by upholding our love for God and for our neighbor as ourselves. I won't go into anything further in Bible study than focus on how these two commandments not only govern how I look at some of the issues we face today as a society but also by adhering to these two greatest commandments, as part of my Biblical worldview, such faith in Jesus not as my teacher of these two commandments but more as my Savior and the Lord of my life makes me more of a conservative by today's worldly standards, including within the Black community.

To love God with all of your heart and with all your soul and with all your mind, to me, first of all, means to fear God. Yes, I fear my Creator who created all things on this Earth and beyond it, and as the Bible shares in plenty of occasions, God is powerful enough to do anything that He wants, including punishing the sinful, which would make me fear Him like a son fearing his father when he has done wrong. At the same time, **what I believe is missing among many of those who believe in God, including Christians, is the fear of God, particularly a fear that takes God seriously**. Many of us in our world simply do not take God seriously, as well as His Word, despite what the Bible shares with us as a part of our history. If I truly love God, I will take what He says seriously. **If I truly love God with all of my heart, soul, and mind, I will do my best, in response to His love for me, to uphold His commandments to the best of my ability because He wants me to flourish as a human by His plans and design.** As I have mentioned before, God has been too good for me to not do my best each day to demonstrate my love in response to all He has done for me. **How I look at some of the issues of today and how I would respond to them often comes down to asking myself the question: "What is the best way for me to honor and love God regarding this particular issue?"** By trusting that what God says in His Word is right, and anything outside of His Word that contradicts it is wrong, I am loving God with all that I have, for my fear of God trumps my fear of man. **I seek to honor, respect and**

love God by providing a response to the worldly issues of today that is most consistent to what His Word says that we should do as His children.

To love your neighbor as yourself is to love how God created you as well as your fellow neighbor. I believe that we are all God's creation, whether or not we all subscribe to the same beliefs about God and His love for us. With that said, to hate someone else is to hate what God has created. To hate what God has created is similar to hating what God created in me. Granted, we are all sinful human beings that need a Savior. At the same time, **every one of us — regardless of our differences on the outside or the inside of us — has inherent value to God, deserving of our respect, dignity and love**. To love my neighbor as myself means that I would want the best for someone else as I would for myself. What I know to be best for me to flourish on Earth is what I would wish for others to have as well. Beyond anything else, material or otherwise, I strongly desire every person I encounter on Earth to have a lifelong relationship with Jesus Christ. Such a relationship has benefits that go beyond the short lifetime we live here, while, at the same time, provides us comfort and guidance during the life we walk on Earth. My love for God and for His people is not meant to be kept a secret within me. This passion of mine is meant to be shared boldly, even when I may feel timid inside. Why? Because of the love God has for me and what I have experienced thus far in Jesus is something that I do not want to be selfish to keep to myself. In fact, God commands me, among other Bible-believing Christians to go and make disciples as part of the Great Commission in Matthew 28:16-20.

How does this relate to some of the pressing issues today and how does this make me a conservative? In our world today, with social media, smartphones, and endless ways of entertaining ourselves at home, we are among one of the loneliest generations in time. **It is much easier to go about life, minding your own business, especially when you can catch a lot of flack from others, when you try to share how your way of viewing the world may benefit someone else. As it was in the days of biblical times, many people want to be wise in their own eyes and do what they feel is right, even if that is against what God had originally intended when He created us. When I view some of the issues of today, I look at them not only in what is best for me to respond as an act of love towards God but also what is loving – with grace and truth – towards my neighbor, whether he or she is a believer or not.** Holding true to the Bible as my compass, despite it being thousands of years old in coverage and has stood the test of time for hundreds of years through numerous past generations of human beings, is a conservative way to look at life as opposed to adopting newer alternative ways of living life, which may include a "do you" philosophy, where no one should judge – or constructively comment – on how you go about living your life, as long as it does not hurt anybody and that you have gotten consent from anyone you participate in activities with. To want what is best for me includes wanting what is best for others. That is part of what it means to love your neighbor as you love yourself.

With all that being said, this is just the appetizer as the introduction. Let's dig into the main course now.

IDENTITY ANCHORED IN FAITH, NOT FLESH

The pale glow of dawn filtered through the stained-glass window of the old church, painting the pews with muted hues of hope. Jacob, a middle-aged man with thoughtful eyes that had seen more than they cared to, rested his elbows on a worn oak pew, his face a mosaic of conflicted emotions. He had always wrestled with the complexities of identity — where did his faith end, and the color of his skin begin?

As sunlight whispered secrets onto the ancient stone floor, Jacob sifted through the tapestry of his memories, each thread a story of belonging and alienation, unity and strife. He had been born in a family where skin color marked your place in the world, your community; your possibilities bounded by the perceptions of others. Now, as he held his grandmother's worn Bible in his hands, he wondered if the pages within could offer a different narrative.

Jacob's mind wandered to a conversation he once had, where words like 'salvation' and 'new creation' were punctuated with conviction.

Those words had pulled at something deep within him, hinting at an identity so profound, it transcended the labels that had adhered to him like a second skin. He recollected a passage, "Therefore, if anyone is in Christ, he is a new creation. The old has passed away; behold, the new has come." The new — how he yearned for that freedom from the fetters of societal categorizations.

A child's laughter outside interrupted his introspection, reminding him of his own children and the world he wanted for them—a world where faith would inform who they were, more than the shades of their skin. He imagined what it'd be like to prioritize this identity in Christ, to let the implicit understanding of his inherent worth in God's eyes inform his business decisions, his views on politics, his interactions with his neighbors.

Yet doubt cast a long shadow in the corners of Jacob's mind. Could embracing this Christ-centered identity truly reconcile the divisions around him, could it heal wounds and bridge the gaps? His heart held the hope of unity found in the vast body of believers worldwide, a unity not confined by physical borders or racial divides, but shaped by a shared faith.

There, in the quiet sanctuary, bombarded by the cacophony of chirping birds and the resonance of his own heart's rhythm, Jacob closed his eyes. He pictured himself rising above the fragments of a fractured society, anchored by a faith that promised wholeness.

How would Jacob's reborn conviction in his faith challenge the labels the world had stamped on him, and what impact would this reshaped identity have on the tangible world he navigated each day?

Unshackled Identities: The Liberation of Faith

In an era where external labels seek dominion over inner truths, the Black Christian journey unfolds as a testament to the power of faith in shaping identity. It is here, at the nexus of spirituality and selfhood, that one may uncover a transformative process — a shift from the temporal to the eternal in defining who we are. This poignant evolution from identifying with the world to finding a home in faith serves as the cornerstone of our conversation.

Understanding how Christian faith redefines personal identity becomes more than a philosophical inquiry; it is a journey towards liberation from the constraints of race and societal expectations. **As black Christians delve deeper into Scripture, the teachings of Jesus Christ call for a profound re-examination of the premises upon which they build their identities.** This is not just a reprioritization but a rebirth, where faith identity emerges paramount, offering a foundation more enduring than the sands of social and racial categorization.

Within these pages lies an exploration of the implications of prioritizing faith identity. This terrain, though less traveled, speaks to the courage required to defy convention. It echoes the stories of Daniel, who stood unwavering in the den of lions, and Moses, who led his people out of Egypt guided by unwavering conviction. The reader embarks on a journey that takes them beyond the flesh, teaching that it is in the spiritual anchorage that one finds true character and calling.

Faith as a primary identifier does not seek to erase one's cultural or racial backdrop but to transcend it, allowing these aspects to become part of a larger, more harmonious portrait. It challenges the reader to **examine scriptural references supporting identity**

based primarily on a relationship with Jesus Christ. Paul's letter to the Galatians resounds with relevance, stating, "There is neither Jew nor Greek, there is neither slave nor free, there is no male and female, for you are all one in Christ Jesus" (Galatians 3:28). This biblical truth underpins the resolve to see oneself through the lens of faith first.

This chapter nudges the reader towards an intersection of spiritual awakening and political consciousness. Insights from theology, politics, and economics interweave to present a canvas where the conservation of one's faith-anchored identity is in concert with the beat of community life. It urges readers to recognize their political orientations might shift, not based on societal trends but driven by a biblically informed worldview.

Embarking on this course demands a fortitude that is both personal and collective. **It requires a steadfast dedication to one's beliefs and values in the face of a world that often dismisses conservatism, especially within the context of the Black community.** Here, we uncover the importance of community — a collective bond strengthened, not weakened, by the shared courage of individual convictions.

This chapter serves as a gateway, opening into a series of reflections and strategies that further unpack how to live authentically within the realms of faith and politics as a Christian who is also black and conservative. The journey from this point forward will not only redefine identity but will also invite readers to stand firm, fostering a transformation that aligns with Christian values — a hallmark of true freedom.

In an era where identity is often segmented into categories of race, ethnicity, and social status, the Christian faith provides an alternative lens through which we can view ourselves. **The intrinsic value of an individual, as taught in the Gospel, lies not in these transient**

markers but in our inherent worth as children of God. This can be a profound comfort and a radical shift for those who are accustomed to defining themselves primarily by the color of their skin or the socioeconomic rung they occupy.

Christianity ushers in a new identity that supersedes all earthly divisions: it offers a spiritual kinship that binds believers across all man-made boundaries. This identity is deeply rooted in the belief that we are all made in the image of God (*imago Dei*), as stated in Genesis 1:27. **As followers of Christ, we are called to adopt an identity that is anchored in this divine likeness, rather than the classifications that society imposes.**

However, this shift in self-perception doesn't erase the significance of race or social context; it rather encompasses and transcends them. Holding one's faith as the primary identifier does not negate the experiences and cultures that shape us, but instead enriches our interactions within the diverse tapestry of humanity. Within the embrace of Christianity, we find that our personal narratives and our spiritual journeys intertwine, creating a more comprehensive self-understanding.

Diving deeper into the Scriptures provides an inspiring clarity — **our worth is secured by nothing less than the sacrifice of Jesus Christ. This profound realization encourages us to see ourselves and others through a lens of grace and redemption, distilling our complex identities to their purest form: beloved creations of God, called to love and to serve with the gifts we have been given, following the example of the Parable of the Talents.**

This new spiritual identity can be incredibly liberating. **It releases individuals from the pressure to conform to the world's expectations and empowers them to live a life of purpose, guided by the teachings and example of Jesus.** In the pursuit of this

Christ-centered identity, we find that the values we hold dear and the decisions we make — politically, socially, and in business — are also transformed. **Our faith becomes the foundation on which all other aspects of our lives are built, establishing a solid ground from which we can navigate the complexities of the world.**

In the practical realm, embracing a faith-first identity manifests in how we conduct ourselves in our communities and workplaces. One's entrepreneurial endeavors, for instance, might then be imbued with a sense of mission, reflecting Christ's principles in every transaction and interaction. A business run on Christian ethics not only thrives in its integrity but also serves as a beacon of His light in the marketplace.

Beyond Conformity: Aligning Your True Identity with Divine Purpose

The journey to grasp and live out a faith-based identity requires both courage and humility. It invites an ongoing reflection on our choices and lifestyle, ensuring that they correlate with our spiritual values. **It is a call to remain grounded in faith amidst a world of shifting allegiances and fading labels, confidently embracing the timeless identity gifted to us by our Creator.**

When individuals allow their faith to shape their understanding of who they are, they engage in a profound reorientation of identity. For followers of Christ, this process involves placing spiritual identity at the foreground of their self-conception. In practice, this emphasis transforms various aspects of life, from personal relationships to social interactions. **More importantly, it changes the weights we give to different aspects of our identities - race, nationality, or career become secondary to our primary identification as children of God.** By reshaping our perspective, faith allows us to move beyond the confines of earthly labels, offering us a deeper connection to something eternal and immutable.

The Power of Faith as a Primary Identity

In considering our identities as believers, our allegiance to faith takes precedence. This prioritization has substantial implications. Notably, it challenges the societal notion that one's racial or cultural heritage wholly determines identity. Instead, faith identity encourages the discernment of one's values, ethics, and purpose through the lens of Christian belief. This does not negate the importance of our heritage, background, or race, but it situates these within the larger narrative of our faith walk. Viewing ourselves as followers of Christ first and foremost consolidates a sense of belonging and purpose that outstrips societal categorizations.

The Implications for Community and Unity

Prioritizing spiritual identity over other forms of identification also carries potential for unity within the Christian community. **By recognizing our shared identity in Christ, believers of diverse backgrounds can overcome divisions**. This is not simply a theoretical ideal; **it has practical relevance in fostering harmonious relationships across racial and cultural divides**. Our shared values and commitments as Christians provide a foundation for mutual understanding and respect, fortifying the bonds that hold us together as a community of faith.

The Influence on Worldview and Action

Moreover, this redefined identity invariably influences one's world-view and informs action. Individuals who view the world from a faith-first perspective are likely to be guided by principles that reflect their spiritual convictions. This can affect not just personal choices but also one's engagement with societal issues. **A faith-oriented identity encourages a response to the world's challenges that is compassionate, principled, and rooted in the teachings of Jesus Christ.**

The transformation of identity through faith inevitably prompts an assessment of one's political orientation and societal engagement. **As Christians, we are called to be** *"in the world but not of the world,"* **suggesting that our political engagement should be informed more by our faith, rather than partisan ideology.** By reassessing our affiliations through the lens of faith, we develop an approach to politics that seeks the welfare of all people and aligns with divine principles.

The Impact on Leadership and Influence

Embracing faith as a primary identity marker also shapes one's approach to leadership and influence. In business and entrepreneurship, for instance, leaders who are grounded in their spiritual convictions are well-positioned to lead with integrity, ethical decision-making, and a commitment to service. This faith-centered leadership model stands as a compelling testament to the transformative power of a faith-first identity, guiding others by example and inspiring them to also seek value beyond material success.

Navigating the Challenges of Faith-Based Identity

One cannot overlook, however, that living out a faith-based identity can be challenging, particularly in environments that may not understand or value spiritual convictions. Yet, in the face of resistance or misunderstanding, the strength of conviction derived from a faith-anchored identity equips individuals with resilience and fortitude. Persistent commitment to Biblical principles above all serves as an anchor, holding steady against the shifting tides of societal expectations and peer pressures.

A Call to Introspection and Growth

Ultimately, identifying first as a follower of Jesus Christ is not merely a one-time decision but a continual process of introspection and growth. **It is about constantly evaluating how our actions, relationships, and decisions align with our faith.** Such introspection encourages authenticity, allowing us to live not only as we are perceived by others but as we are known by God. This ongoing journey requires diligence, courage, and an openness to being shaped by spiritual truths — qualities that are integral to a mature, reflective faith journey.

We recognize the profound implications of choosing Jesus as the primary axis of our identity. Such a commitment forms a worldview that embraces Biblical principles above societal norms. It calls for a re-examination of our convictions and motivates us to lead lives of greater purpose and unity. While this choice does not eliminate the complexities and challenges inherent in other forms of identification (i.e. race and ethnicity), it provides a robust framework for navigating them. The faith-anchored identity is a bulwark in an ever-changing world — a reminder that our truest sense of self comes not from without, but from within, guided by our relationship with Jesus Christ.

Scriptural Foundations for Identity in Christ

The quest for identity in the modern, fallen world can often feel like navigating an invisible maze, leading many to cling to surface-level identifiers such as race, occupation, or social status. However, for the Christian believer, **the Bible offers a different perspective, one that anchors identity not in the fleeting or divisive, but in something eternal and unifying**. The New Testament, in particular, provides a rich tapestry of verses that speak of a new identity found in Jesus Christ. **Galatians 3:28 says,** *"There is neither Jew nor Gentile, neither slave nor free, nor is there male and female, for you are all one in Christ Jesus."* This emphatically suggests that in God's kingdom, our primary identity is not our ethnicity, gender, or social class, but our unity in Christ.

Understanding this identity requires a different mindset, one that embraces eternal values over temporal accolades. The Apostle Paul exemplifies this when he states in **Philippians 3:20,** *"But our citizenship is in heaven, and from it we await a Savior, the Lord Jesus Christ."* As believers, our true citizenship, and thus our true identity, originates not from the nations we are born into but from the Kingdom of God. This verse also underlines the expectancy and hope that comes with this citizenship — a hope that empowers Christians to live beyond contemporary labels and towards a heavenly promise.

Furthermore, Scriptures counsel believers to don a new self. Ephesians 4:24 advises, *"And to put on the new self, created after the likeness of God in true righteousness and holiness."* **This "new self" is rooted in the character of God, shaped by His righteousness and holi-**

ness, and is a far cry from a self defined by worldly measures of
racial solidarity, success or prestige. This instruction motivates us
to embody qualities that reflect our divine origin, fostering an identity
that is consistent with our Christian faith.

The Transformation Through Christ

In our adoption as children of God, we witness another profound
aspect of our redefined identity. **John 1:12-13 declares, *"But to all
who did receive Him, who believed in His name, He gave the
right to become children of God."*** This adoption transcends all
human prescribed identities, placing us in a family where the bonds
are spiritual rather than biological. **In this familial relationship, our
sense of self widens to include our brothers and sisters in Christ,
creating a global community grounded in spiritual kinship that
surpasses all other surface-level identifiers, including race, gender, and nationality.**

This concept is particularly transformative when considered in the
context of a society where racial and cultural identities can overshadow spiritual ones. **By recognizing our primary identity as children
of God, we are empowered to interact with others from a place
of shared spiritual heritage, which can help break down barriers
that worldly identifiers often erect.** This unity in faith underscores
the fact that while we may have different life experiences and backgrounds, our most defining characteristic is our mutual redemption
and inheritance in Christ.

Living Out Our Identity in Christ

Living out our new identity in Christ is not merely a theological exercise; it is also a practical calling to manifest the teachings of Jesus in every aspect of our lives. The Beatitudes (Matthew 5:3-12), for instance, present a blueprint for Christian living. They teach us that blessedness comes not from worldly affirmation or accomplishments but from demonstrating values such as meekness, righteousness, mercy, purity of heart, and peacemaking. These attributes shape how we engage with the world, casting a Christ-like reflection that supersedes any earthly label.

In the midst of secular pressures and societal expectations, Christians are reminded to stand firm in their divine identity. 1 Peter 2:9 resounds with a powerful call to action, stating, *"But you are a chosen race, a royal priesthood, a holy nation, a people for his own possession, that you may proclaim the excellencies of Him who called you out of darkness into his marvelous light."* This verse not only confirms our chosen status in God's eyes but also impels us to be emissaries of His light and truth.

As stewards of this heavenly calling, believers are thus challenged to continually renew their minds. Romans 12:2 urges, *"Do not conform to the pattern of this world, but be transformed by the renewing of your mind."* Integrating this practice enables us to resist being defined by the world's fleeting standards and instead embrace an identity that is constantly being refined according to God's purposes. It is through this renewal that we can remain steadfast in our convictions and authentically represent our faith in various aspects of society.

An Unshakeable Spiritual Heritage

Our belonging to Christ comes with an unshakeable spiritual heritage that withstands the tests of time and the changing tides of society. Hebrews 12:28 reminds us, *"Therefore let us be grateful for a kingdom that cannot be shaken, and thus let us offer to God acceptable worship, with reverence and awe."* This unshakeable kingdom is the foundation upon which our identity is built. It encourages a gratitude that emanates from recognizing that our identity is grounded in something far more durable and sacred than any worldly accolade or affiliation.

The Bible's metanarrative from Genesis to Revelation is one of identity being found in God's creating, redeeming, and sanctifying work. By accepting this scriptural truth, believers can embody an identity that is anchored in faith — **a faith that not only recognizes them as God's own but also as agents of His transformative love in the world.** This identity supersedes any human categorization, offering a profound sense of belonging and purpose that informs all aspects of life, from personal relationships to community engagement, and from business endeavors to political perspectives.

Redefining Personal Identity Through Faith

Embracing the Christian faith invites us on a journey of self-discovery that transcends conventional racial and societal markers. Through Christ, we find an identity that is not confined by the bounds of flesh but is anchored in the eternal. This foundational truth challenges us to reshape our understanding of who we are and how we engage with the world.

Faith is not just a component of our lives — it is the defining core from which all else emanates. It impacts our personal encounters, our community interactions, and the broader societal discourse. By prioritizing our spiritual identity, we gain a perspective that is refreshingly liberating and profoundly countercultural.

Scriptural Foundations for Identity in Christ

The scriptures offer an undeniable validation of this new identity. They encourage believers to view themselves through the lens of their relationship with Jesus Christ, fostering a sense of belonging that overshadows all other affiliations.

In emphasizing the importance of faith, we are reminded of the Apostle Paul's words: *"Therefore, if anyone is in Christ, he is a new creation; the old has gone, the new has come!" (2 Corinthians 5:17)*. This scriptural cornerstone establishes the transformative influence of embracing a faith that is deeply rooted and all-consuming.

Harnessing Faith for Transformation

With each page turned in this book, our spiritual and political harmony will be examined and strengthened. By harnessing the profound relationship between our faith and daily walk, we launch into a deeper, more resilient engagement with the world — one that is informed by timeless principles rather than fleeting trends.

As you continue this journey through the chapters ahead, anticipate a remarkable fusion of growth, insight, and empowerment. The road may challenge preconceived notions and provoke introspection, but it is designed to fortify your convictions and illuminate your path with clarity and purpose.

This book serves as more than a mere discussion of ideals — it is an interactive guide packed with actionable advice, practical wisdom, and entrepreneurial spirit. It beckons you to step up as leaders and innovators within your communities, businesses, and political spheres, all while upholding the integrity of your Christian faith.

Facing Challenges with Unyielding Conviction

Every chapter will build upon the knowledge that your identity in faith is crucial. It will provide a foundation to withstand the tempests of political and societal pressures. With your identity firmly grounded in Christ, you are equipped to confront challenges with unyielding conviction and grace.

But challenges are merely stepping stones to greater triumphs. They are opportunities to demonstrate the strength of a faith-based identity, to live out the fullness of a life dedicated to biblical principles, and to influence the world from a place of unwavering moral certainty and conviction.

The Journey Ahead

As you embark on the coming chapters, prepare yourself for a transformative experience. You will be presented with strategies to navigate the complexities of conservatism within the experience of being a Christian within the black community. Integrating theological insights, political analysis, and economic principles, the ensuing discussion will offer a tapestry of learning that enriches and inspires.

Allow the text that follows to speak to your heart and mind, urging you on to greater heights. This book is your invitation to engage with a community of believers who, like you, aspire to live authentically at the intersection of faith and real-world application.

The path ahead is one of discovery, engagement, and unapologetic assertion of a Christian-first, conservative-light identity. It is paved with the assurance that your faith is the most profound anchor, and with this certainty, no storm can displace you.

Embrace the journey. Accept the challenge. Step forth with confidence, knowing that the redefinition of your identity is not just a personal victory, but a testament to the transformative power of faith.

UNVEILING SCRIPTURAL CONSERVATISM IN PROGRESSIVE HAVENS

In the small town of Maplewood, sunlight filtered through the stained-glass windows of a quaint old church, casting mosaics of color upon its aged pews. Johnathan, a pillar of this tiny community and its spiritual heart, sat alone on one of those rigid oaken benches — a Bible rested in his hands, its edges worn from use. His gaze traced the well-trodden verses, seeking guidance amidst an internal struggle that lays heavy upon his soul.

Maplewood had always been a landscape of traditional values, where the roots of belief ran as deep as the towering oaks that lined its quiet streets. Johnathan's faith was unequivocal, a beacon that shone through his every action. Yet, the winds of cultural and societal change gusted through the town, bringing with them ideas that clashed with the time-honored principles he held dear. Johnathan's conscience grappled with the breadth of shifting thought within his beloved community, where liberal ideologies had begun to take hold.

How could he maintain his steadfastness to the doctrine that framed his existence?

The murmurs of the past whispered in his ear, evoking times when biblical teachings were the compass by which all decisions were navigated. His heart clenched at the thought of dissent, of standing firm against the tide. Yet, he pondered the parables of old, understanding that they anchored him to a conservative stance, one out of step with many around him. The dilemma was clear: could his faith remain resolute without creating rifts in the fabric of his friendships, his family, and his community?

A child's laughter erupted outside, slicing through the meditative silence of the church, reminding him that the world moved inexorably forward, whether in tandem with Scripture or in its own spirited (or secular) dance. Johnathan's eyes lifted to observe through the church's open door; the vibrant lives unfurling beyond its sanctuary. There was a humble beauty in their innocent divergence from his own path, a reminder that love must knit together the frayed edges of discord.

Closing the sacred text, Johnathan rose and stepped out into the golden wash of the afternoon. Life in Maplewood went about its business — people greeted him warmly, respecting the faith he bore like a shield. Yet, he wondered, as he walked past the bustling marketplace and lively debates spilling from the town's café, was it possible to bridge the gap between old and new, to foster mutual understanding within the diversity of conviction?

His stride carried him towards the heart of the town, where decisions were made, and futures shaped. Today, among friends and neighbors, they would discuss the latest policy being introduced — a test of tolerance and testaments. It was there, in the meeting hall, that Johnathan planned to tender his perspective, one molded by Scripture and, consequently, conservative ideals. He would listen, learn, and lead by example, hoping to illustrate that faith need not be embattled but could guide gently with wisdom and grace.

The scent of freshly mown grass filled his senses, an earthy reminder of life's perpetuity, and the faith that everything had its season. The community hall loomed ahead, its doors ajar, a symbol to all that they were welcome. Each step he took was a prayer, each breath a testament to his resolve. Could Johnathan, with his deep-rooted beliefs, steer the discourse towards reconciliation, towards a future where differing views might coexist in respect and harmony?

Within the confines of that meeting room, how would the words of an ancient text resonate with his community, and could the serenity that comes with true faith light the way for others around him?

The Inconspicuous Bond Between Faith and Conservatism

The journey of Black Christians through the political landscape has often been one of aligning with liberal ideologies, assumed to be inherently supportive of their struggles and aspirations. However, **a closer examination of the principles that guide their faith reveals that many of these teachings align closely with conservative values.** The intersection of Christianity with conservative ideology is more seamless, compared to that with liberal ideology, when scriptural backing is at the forefront of societal norms and personal convictions. It is within this context that individuals may discover a conservatism that not only resonates with their spiritual beliefs but also provides a more Biblical framework for engaging with the world.

This chapter navigates the intricate paths that connect the dots between scriptural teachings and conservative philosophies. Drawing from both sacred texts and modern life, it is apparent that **an adher-**

ence to Christian principles often fosters a more conservative perspective. Though this may appear at odds with the broader narrative, it illuminates the diversity of thought within the Black community. Realizing how Christian principles can underpin conservative values is pivotal in understanding one's personal political compass.

The challenges of adopting conservative viewpoints within traditionally liberal communities are manifold. **Doing so can lead to a sense of isolation or the perception of betrayal. However, it is crucial to acknowledge that embracing conservative values does not necessitate abandoning one's cultural or communal identity. Rather, it calls for boldness in standing firm in one's convictions while navigating the nuances and expectations of one's surroundings.** This part of the journey requires courage, wisdom, and an unwavering faith in the guiding tenets of Christianity.

Biblical precedents that underpin conservative ideologies are numerous and compelling. They offer a historical and theological foundation for values such as family unity, personal responsibility, and ethical integrity. By analyzing scriptural guidance on these issues, believers may find themselves affirming traditional conservative positions. It is not a simple confluence of religious adherence and political stance but a well-reasoned alignment that emerges from a more comprehensive understanding of biblical doctrines.

To fully comprehend this shift in perspective, one must engage with the Bible actively and reflect on its timeless wisdom in context to present-day quandaries. Valuable insights can be gained from the theological underpinnings of conservative thought, especially when these ideas are applied to areas such as economics, community structure, and social welfare. It is a testament to the dynamic nature of faith that such interpretations can validate a conservative worldview.

In navigating the dual identities of being both Black and Christ-ian, and potentially conservative, there is richness in dialogue, under-standing, and unity in diversity. While this can be an uncomfortable process, it is essential for the individual journey and the collective evolution of the community. As such, it is a process that demands not only intellectual engagement but also an openness to spiritual guidance and personal growth.

The quest for coherence between one's faith and political beliefs is not a departure from the essence of the Black Christian experience. It is, in fact, a continuation of a historical pursuit of authenticity and truth. Those who find themselves on this path are not anomalies; they are a reflection of the ability of the Black church and its congregation to wrestle with and embrace a complex and multifaceted existence. It is a call to evaluate one's principles, engage in meaningful discourse, and uphold the values that resonate deeply with one's spiritual and moral compass.

In walking the path of faith, adherence to Christian principles often takes one on an unexpected trajectory where personal belief intersects with political persuasion. The convictions that arise from rigorous scriptural diligence have the capacity to instill conservative values that may seem at odds with the ideologies of more progressive and liberal communities. The realization dawns slowly, as you find that ancient parables from the Bible hold resonances with contemporary issues around family, work, and societal responsibility.

The Christian narrative champions principles such as the sanctity of life, the importance of family and marriage, and the call to personal stewardship over one's resources. These values, deeply rooted in Scrip-ture, echo throughout halls of conservative thought. When one views these tenets not simply as moral suggestions but as divine imperatives, the shift towards more conservative viewpoints becomes less a choice and more a faithful response to the Gospel's call.

Personal testimony plays a significant role in illustrating how scriptural devotion shapes one's worldview. You might recall instances where decisions grounded in your Christian faith — perhaps on matters of fiscal prudence or ethical integrity in business — aligned more with conservative discourse. These moments highlight the deep connection between the adherence to religious teachings and the advocacy for policies and practices reminiscent of conservative philosophy.

Let us consider the biblical concept of stewardship. The parable of the talents, found in the Gospel of Matthew, serves as a potent metaphor for responsible economic management. It advocates for the wise and fruitful use of resources, a principle that resonates with conservative views on fiscal responsibility and the ethics of capitalism. Viewing one's financial success as a means of glorifying God, and not purely as personal gain, casts economic policy in a light that is distinctly conservative yet firmly based in Christian teachings.

Moreover, the biblical definition of family constitutes a cornerstone for many conservative principles. In communities where liberal ideologies predominate, espousing the traditional view on marriage as defined within Scripture can be contentious. Yet for those deeply committed to their faith, the concept of marriage as a union between a man and a woman ordained by God remains non-negotiable. Conservative values are thus often not a political posture but a lived expression of one's fidelity to Biblical precepts.

It is essential to recognize, however, that Christian conservatism is not monolithic; it allows for a nuanced understanding of Scripture as it applies to modern life. While some may use faith to justify rigid dogmatism, the heart of Christian conservatism seeks to apply ancient wisdom to today's complex moral landscapes. In areas such as social justice and caring for the marginalized — ideals deeply embedded in Christianity—it aligns with elements typically associated with progressive thought while maintaining a conservative framework.

The transformative power of Scripture encompasses the entire spectrum of life's concerns — extending beyond personal spirituality into the realms of governance, economics, and community engagement. As you pore over the historical narratives, proverbs, psalms and teachings of the Bible, the sense of guiding providence often leads to the embrace of conservative tenets that affirm the value of tradition, the rule of law, and the sacredness of individual liberty as seen through the lens of divine intention.

In navigating the intricate relationship between faith and politics, authentic introspection is vital. The examination of how closely one's political beliefs are tied to the core of their religious convictions can be surprisingly revelatory. Embracing this intertwined spiritual-political identity does not necessitate walking away from one's roots; rather, it involves harmonizing ancient scriptural wisdom with contemporary conservatism, recognizing that these principles may serve as a bridge rather than a barricade.

Exploring the Road Less Traveled: Conservative Viewpoints Amidst A More Liberal and Secular World

The Challenge of Nonconformity

When one grounds their life in the foundational truths of the Christian faith, a conservative worldview often takes root, which can seem at odds with the common ethos of "progressive" environments. This divergence can manifest in the emergence of tension and outright conflict, as the values upheld by a Biblical understanding appear to contradict the liberal narrative prevalent within many communities, including those within the Black church. The challenge is not merely ideological but deeply personal, requiring steadfast courage to stand by one's convictions.

Core beliefs can become social fault lines, with the potential to alienate even the most integrated individuals from their communities. It's a reality that faith-filled people face when their scriptural interpretations guide them towards principle-based stances on societal issues such as sanctity of life, God's view on marriage, and personal responsibility. This natural alignment with conservative principles can lead to a sense of isolation, as it may be misconstrued as a betrayal of a collective standpoint.

Embracing Discordance

Adopting conservative viewpoints is to walk a path less traveled within typically liberal circles. It demands resilience to not only hold but also voice opinions that diverge markedly from the consensus. There's a fine balance to be struck between engendering respectful dialogue and upholding one's beliefs without capitulating to the pressure to conform. **This is especially poignant within Black communities, where a rich tapestry of shared history and struggle often dictates a homogeneous political and social outlook.**

Maintaining individual beliefs amid a chorus of opposing voices is a testament to the strength of one's convictions. It requires an understanding that **fellowship need not necessitate uniformity of thought, and that diversity of opinion is a hallmark of a vibrant**

and mature community. Notably, it's in such environments that conservation of faith-based values becomes an act of quiet rebellion, a conscious choice to prioritize the eternal over the ephemeral.

Standing Firm in Conviction

The difficulties in navigating these waters are heightened by the expectation of solidarity in thought and action, especially, in this situation, due to the color of your skin. There is immense pressure to acquiesce to prevailing ideologies within traditionally liberal groups, which can turn philosophical disagreements into personal standoffs. And yet, within these challenges lie opportunities for growth and the deepening of one's faith journey. **To stand firm in conviction is to honor the integrity of one's beliefs and the Word of God that informs them.**

Life's tough choices often reveal the depth of our principles: where do we ultimately seek guidance, and upon what truthful foundation do we build our viewpoints? The discomfort endured through disagreement is a refining fire, one which can solidify our understanding and appreciation for the bedrock tenets of our faith.

The Necessity of Dialogue

Part of navigating the conservative spectrum within these communities entails fostering dialogue, rooted in kindness, curiosity and mutual respect. It is crucial to articulate one's views with clarity, grounded in spiritual teachings, while remaining open to the perspectives of others. The ability to engage in exchange without animosity speaks to Christian principles of love and patience, illustrating that varied viewpoints can coexist within the same space.

The Bible says in 1 Peter 3:15-16: *"But in your hearts re-vere Christ as Lord. Always be prepared to give an answer to everyone who asks you to give the reason for the hope that you have. But do this with gentleness and respect, keeping a clear conscience, so that those who speak maliciously against your good behavior in Christ may be ashamed of their slander."*

The power of discourse lies not only in the exchange of ideas but also in the demonstration of a lived example of scriptural conservatism done with grace and humility. It can bridge the gap between differing ideologies, while also showing reverence for one's own deeply held beliefs.

Leadership by Example

Taking on a leadership role may not always be about guiding the majority; **sometimes, it's about setting an example for the minority who shares your perspective**. It's about creating a space where conservative thought and biblical fidelity are not just tolerated but actively respected, an enclave within the broader community where one's spiritual values are in harmony with their political sentiments.

Leadership in this context does not demand loudness, but rather the quiet strength of consistency and the embodiment of principles in daily life. The impact of living true to one's beliefs can resonate far more profoundly than any argument or debate. It is in the steady, daily application of faith through your actions that the most persuasive sermon is preached.

The Potential for Transformation

Despite the apparent uphill struggle, there is a noble pursuit in the embracing of conservative tenets within progressive societies. **It's a calling that beckons the believer to remain true to his or her faith against the backdrop of ideological contention and peer pressure**. The potential for transformation lies in the ability to view these challenges not as insurmountable obstacles, but as avenues for demonstrating the transformative power of Biblical principles in action.

As agents of change, individuals can lean on their faith to navigate the complexities of aligning conservative values with a progressive environment. In doing so, they present **the possibility for a nuanced understanding that values both tradition and thoughtful progress**. The change might be incremental, but it anchors the hope for a community that can embrace the richness of diverse thought inspired by a shared faith.

The Journey Continues

Every chapter in the story of faith and politics is a lesson in persistence and grace. It's a testament to the enduring spirit of those who choose the road less traveled, who live out their conservatism against the grain of conventional thought in their communities. This path, punctuated by moments of strife and solidarity, continues to unfold as believers seek to reconcile their spiritual convictions with their sociopolitical contexts.

The journey is ongoing, a narrative of individuals holding fast to the Bible that transcends time and culture, while navigating the human condition and its complexities of the here and now. Their living example is a beacon for others, who might quietly share these convictions, to step forward and walk in fellowship, uniting faith and worldview in a seamless tapestry that honors both heritage and personal beliefs.

The Scriptural Roots of Conservatism

Conservatism, at its heart, is a commitment to traditional values and institutions. The Bible, as the infallible, inerrant and objective Word of God and the cornerstone of Christian faith, encompasses numerous teachings that lay the foundation for conservative thought. For example, the concept of stewardship found in the creation mandate (Genesis 1:28) entrusts humans with the care of the earth, reflective of the conservative emphasis on personal responsibility. Meanwhile, the Ten Commandments (Exodus 20) convey the importance of structure and respect for law and order — tenets highly regarded within conservative ideology.

Principles of family and marriage are another domain where scriptural teachings intersect with conservative views. Scriptures such as Ephesians 5:22-33 delineate a traditional view of the nuclear family and marriage, which conservatives often advocate for, underscoring the stability these structures provide. Reliance on Biblical instructions for life's organization is not just a spiritual practice but also a blueprint that shapes the outlook for many conservatives today.

Fiscal Prudence through Biblical Wisdom

The parables of Jesus often encapsulate the virtues of prudence and wise stewardship of resources. The Parable of the Talents (Matthew 25:14-30), for instance, commends the servants who invest and multiply their talents, which aligns with the conservative principle of economic responsibility and the value of hard work. As followers of Christ seek to apply these teachings in modern times, they find a resonance within conservative ideals that advocate for fiscal responsibility and entrepreneurial spirit.

Moreover, the Bible promotes giving to those in need (Proverbs 19:17) but also emphasizes the importance of work (2 Thessalonians 3:10). This balance between charity and personal accountability is a nuanced perspective often echoed in conservative circles, advising a small but sufficient welfare system that empowers individuals rather than creates dependency on the government.

The Sanctity of Life and Scriptural Affirmation

One of the most vivid intersections of Biblical teaching with conservative ideology is the sanctity of life. Passages such as Psalm 139:13-16, which speaks of God's knowledge of us even within the womb, provide a strong scriptural backing to the pro-life stance commonly associated with conservative values. The reverence for life is not merely a theological concept but also forms the basis of conservative advocacy for policies that seek to protect human life at all stages from womb to tomb.

Respect for tradition and authority, as seen in biblical passages that encourage honoring the wisdom of one's parents (Proverbs 1:8-9), is another facet where Christianity and conservatism find common ground. Conservatives draw on this principle to venerate historical institutions and practices that have withstood the test of time, consistent with scriptural teachings.

Governance and Divine Ordinance

The Apostle Paul's exhortation in Romans 13:1-7 to respect governing authorities has been interpreted as a support for law and order — a hallmark of conservative thought. **The Bible does not shy away from the idea of a structured society governed by laws that are just and leaders who are accountable to divine will under the authority of God.** Such scriptural precedents can lead Christians to value a political system that upholds order, justice, and freedom, pillars also celebrated by conservatism.

Freedom of Belief Anchored in Scripture

Freedom of religion, a critical component of conservative ideology, is also deeply embedded in the Christian faith. The New Testament narrative champions an individual's right to belief and conversion, as seen in the book of Acts and the epistles. This autonomy in matters of faith is analogized within conservative thought as the individual's freedom to choose and live out their convictions without undue constraint from others and the government.

The Consistency of Moral Law

Moral absolutes are a common theme throughout Scripture. **From the laws given on Mount Sinai to the moral teachings of Jesus in the Sermon on the Mount, the Bible presents a case for absolute truth that transcends cultural changes.** This idea, that moral truths are eternal, also permeates conservative philosophy, which resists moral relativism and upholds the idea of unwavering moral principles.

Practical Faith in Daily Affairs

Christians are encouraged to live out their faith in every aspect of their lives — not just in religious observance, but also in their professional and community engagements. The Apostle James challenges believers to show their faith through their actions (James 2:14-26). This active faith can inform a conservative lifestyle, one that integrates Christian principles into daily decision-making processes, business dealings, family teachings, and social interactions.

Combining a spiritual mandate with practical application, adherents of scriptural conservatism find themselves operating in a manner that is not only principled but also socially and economically proactive. In many ways, these enduring principles serve as a compass for navigating the complicated terrain of modern political and societal landscapes.

Embracing Principles for a Conservative Outlook

Adherence to Christian values often leads one to conservative viewpoints, reflecting a profound respect for scriptural teachings. This chapter aimed to demonstrate that when individuals engage deeply with Biblical principles, a conservative perspective can naturally emerge. Even within traditionally liberal spaces, such values stand firm, challenging norms and encouraging dialogue. The crux of this worldview is the reliance on timeless spiritual wisdom to offer stability and clarity to navigate faithfully through the ever-changing complexities of modern social and political landscapes in our fallen and sinful world.

Upholding Values Amongst Diverse Voices

In diverse communities, where the chorus of ideas is strong and varied, standing firm in one's convictions requires both courage and nuance. Our shared humanity and the manifold expressions of faith provide common ground, while our respectful assertiveness in matters of principle carves out space for conservative values to be heard and considered. It is possible to honor one's personal convictions without diminishing the beliefs of others, paving the way for a tapestry of viewpoints to coexist harmoniously.

Motivation to Act

Let us therefore aspire not only to appreciate the intricate weaving of faith and conservatism but to become architects of change within our spheres of influence - ourselves, our families, our places of worship, our schools, our workplaces, our friends, our organizations, and our communities. Regardless of our communal settings, we are called to action – to demonstrate the efficacy of Biblically rooted conservatism through our lives and works. It is in living out these principles consistently and daily that we bear witness to their value, inspiring others to reflect upon their own positions and the greater impact on our communities.

Nurturing Connection Through Shared Experience

Drawing from our own narratives and the collective wisdom of those who have walked similar paths, we find a sense of camaraderie. Personal stories not only humanize the seemingly abstract but also act as a conduit for shared understanding and growth. Through vulnerability and authenticity, we strengthen the connection with our readers, emboldening them to forge their own journey with confidence.

Striking the Right Chord

In our discourse, we must balance the authoritative with the accessible, imparting knowledge that resonates and empowers. It is through sincerity and genuine engagement that our message resonates most deeply. Let us strive to speak with an assured yet inviting tone, fostering not merely adherence but thoughtful consideration and personal conviction.

Conclusion

Through the lens of the varied Black Christian experience, we have scrutinized the compelling relationship between faith and conservatism. We are reminded that Biblical principles can underlie our worldview, guiding not only our spiritual endeavors but our societal engagements as well. As we marinate on this chapter's discourse, let the principles espoused herein not simply inform us but propel us forward in our quest for a life – and community – anchored in enduring Biblical truth.

SYNCHRONIZING SOUL AND SOCIETY

The sun had yet to claim its throne in the early morning sky when Sarah stepped outside, the cool tendrils of dawn's breath winding around her like a familiar shawl. She had always appreciated these solitary moments before the world awoke; it was in these silences that the whispers of her soul often spoke loudest. Her footsteps were steady against the cobblestone path leading through the heart of the small town, each echo a testament to the years she'd spent weaving her faith into the fabric of this place.

As she neared the corner bakery, the sweet aroma of freshly baked bread wafted through the air, a simple yet profound reminder of daily sustenance, both physical and spiritual. Sarah had long sought to embody the principles of her belief — compassion, integrity, service — in her every interaction within this community. Yet, beneath her serene exterior swirled a conflict, a rising tide questioning if her efforts to live authentically among her neighbors truly mirrored the depth of her internal Christian convictions.

The jingle of the bakery door pulled her from her reverie, a gentle yet firm summons to the present. Inside, the baker, Mrs. Thomas, greeted her with a smile that reached her eyes, a genuine extension of warmth, as she handed Sarah a loaf, still warm to the touch. The exchange was mundane in its routine, yet it held an undercurrent of something greater; for Sarah, it was an act of witnessing, a demonstration of shared humanity that transcended a mere transaction.

And yet, as Sarah continued along her path, making her way towards the market square, she was vividly aware of the eyes that followed her — not with malice but with a curiosity that yearned for congruence between her spoken faith and her lived experience. As the town gradually awoke, the tapestry of life weaving itself anew, she pondered how best to reconcile her private devotion with the public square, to align her inward spirituality with outward action, in a manner both seamless and sincere.

Lingering amidst the throb of bargaining and banter at the market, she listened, not just to the words but to the stories beneath them, the shared struggles and victories that colored every human interaction. Against the canvas of commerce and monetary exchange, she understood that her role was not to stand apart but to step into the fray, embodying grace, leading by subtle example, building trust through steadfastness, compassion and consistency.

As she paused, amidst the undulating waves of conversation that washed over the expanse of stalls and stands, was it enough, Sarah wondered, to perform acts of kindness and speak words of faith, or did authenticity demand a deeper fusion of belief and behavior, one that beckoned even when no eyes bore witness? How could her every step, every word, every silence, echo the profound yet simple truth that the fabric of her being was indelibly woven with threads of divine purpose? Could she inspire others to realize that the mosaic of their lives, too, was a masterpiece of co-created beauty, desperately needed in the gallery of the world?

Unearthing the Rhythms of Integrity

Living an authentic life is not just a luxury; it is an imperative that calls for the deep intertwining of our spiritual beliefs with our earnest involvement in society. It is here, at the crossroads of soul and society, where Black Christians walking the conservative path find themselves grappling with a profound truth: a life fragmented between personal faith and public engagement is a life fraught with incongruity. The melody of one's existence gains harmony only when the notes of faith and civic action are synchronized into a coherent and melodious whole.

This universal struggle for authenticity becomes particularly poignant within the Black Christian community. Tradition and innovation, reverence and progress, community and the individual, all are held in balance by an ever-present faith. However, for the conservative Black Christian, the complexities multiply. In a society that often equates conservatism with opposition to racial progress, the challenge to remain true to both one's faith and socio-political convictions can be formidable. Herein lies the journey we embark upon — one that demands not just understanding, but masterful coordination, of the symphony of one's beliefs and actions.

The Quest for Authenticity

The quest for authenticity requires us to focus laser-like on our core values, using them as a compass to navigate the waters of societal engagement. We must endeavor to demonstrate our Christian convictions not only within the pews of our churches but within the bustling marketplaces of our communities. To cultivate a life that is anchored in faith yet active in societal transformation, there must be a deliberate effort to transcend the dichotomy often laid before us, bridging the gap between the spiritual and the social.

Strategies for Integration

Identifying strategies for integrating Christian conservatism into our daily lives marks the beginning of this transformative process. This chapter deliberates on not just the 'why' but also the 'how'. It is about making the abstract tangible, the theoretical practical. Each strategy detailed is a thread in the tapestry we seek to weave—a tapestry that envisions communities bolstered by morally grounded, politically aware, and active individuals.

Maintaining Integrity in Dual Realms

To maintain integrity in both our private and public personas, the harmonization of soul and society is non-negotiable. It is through the daily practice of this harmony that Black Christians can stand firm against the tides of an ever-evolving political and social landscape. As we reflect on practical ways to sustain this unity of purpose and identity, we move beyond mere compliance to an embodiment of authenticity in every sense.

The Conservatism Confluence Process

The goal of the **Conservatism Confluence Process** is to guide you, the reader, to a place where your conservative values and Christian faith not only coexist but deepen each other — a confluence of two compelling forces in your life that gives rise to an authentic and powerful witness to the world.

Reflect on Your Values

Begin by allocating time to introspection, to ponder the values that form the bedrock of your identity. Contemplate on Judeo-Christian values, love for God and for one another, and personal responsibility—values that dovetail with conservative principles. Make a personal inventory of these core values. This reflection is not a hurried task; give it the gravitas it deserves, for it sets the foundation for your journey.

Study Conservative Ideology

Dedicate time to understand conservatism from the inside out. Engage with the writings and thoughts of conservative thought leaders and intellectuals, immerse in discussions that challenge and refine your perspectives. This educational pilgrimage aims to equip you with a philosophical map of the conservative terrain.

Examine Your Faith

In the examination of your faith, study the Bible to seek out the harmonies and tensions with conservatism. Faith is not a static component; it is vibrant and often intersects with the principles you uphold in the political realm. This step is an exploration of fusion points - identifying where your spiritual journey informs and enhances your political stance.

Identify Potential Conflicts

Recognize and confront discrepancies head-on. Analyzing these points of divergence is crucial because it demands authenticity and fosters growth. Expect this part of the process to be uncomfortable but restorative, like the refining of gold.

Seek Spiritual Guidance

Harness wisdom from trusted spiritual mentors to navigate the complex interplay between your beliefs and Scripture. Such guidance is invaluable, providing a lantern to light your path when the reconciliation between faith and conservatism seems obscured.

Reflect on Personal Experiences

Your journey is yours alone, marked by unique experiences that influence your worldview. Reflect upon the intertwining of your faith and political stances across your life's narrative, recognizing how these life experiences have shaped you.

Create a Personal Manifesto

Articulate your convictions in a personal manifesto — an organized and succinct declaration of the principles that you pledge to live by. This document is both a mirror reflecting your beliefs and a map guiding your actions. Make sure that it is biblical in nature and that it does not contradict the Word of God.

Regularly Revisit and Refine

Your manifesto is not set in stone. As you venture forth, routinely return to it for reflection and refinement as you engage further with the Bible. Allow your understanding to evolve while clutching firmly to the values that reconcile your faith with your conservative ethos.

The success of the Conservatism Confluence Process is measured not just by its completion, but by the continuous integration of its principles into the fabric of your life. It goes beyond the pages of this book into the lived reality of your daily walk, solidifying your resolve to live authentically at the intersection of faith and society.

Authentic living reaches its fullest expression when an individual's internal beliefs and external actions become one. For those walking a path lit by the Christian faith, reconciling spiritual convictions with societal duties is not negotiable — it is essential. In a world where personal integrity often battles against social conformity, **Christians are called to be the salt and light of the world (Matthew 5:13-16); preserving and revealing God's grace in every aspect of life.** This harmonization of soul and society ensures the seamless embodiment of Christian values, whether we are within the walls of our churches or out in the broader community.

Achieving this integration starts with a clear understanding of Christian values and how they apply beyond personal spirituality.

Love, righteousness, justice, compassion, and humility, for example, are not merely concepts to be contemplated but are principles to be practiced. These cornerstones of Christian doctrine directly influence how one engages with the world—whether it's in fostering community relations, participating in politics, or pursuing entrepreneurial ventures. When these values are deeply embedded in our actions, we consistently affirm our identity as believers not only in word but also in deed.

But navigating this confluence of faith and life demands more than just abstract knowledge. It requires practical strategies and regular spiritual disciplines to build a life that does not separate Sunday reflections from Monday - Saturday actions. Intentional incorporation of prayer, Bible study, weekly small group gatherings, and a commitment to Godly living form the bedrock of an authentic Christian lifestyle. As one's spiritual foundation strengthens, the decisions made in business and community interactions reflect a cohesive moral compass.

Moreover, authenticity as a Christian in society is not synonymous with perfection. It is about striving towards consistency and transparency in one's beliefs and actions to **be more like Jesus Christ** than before. Open acknowledgement of one's faith can serve as a guidepost for others who might be seeking direction in a perplexing world. By demonstrating integrity in both successes and failures, publicly and privately, believers can offer real-world testimonies to the transformative power of living a faith-centered life that honors God.

Implementing such a faith-based worldview does not exist without challenge, especially within diverse communities where Christian conservative views may clash with prevailing social ideologies. The pressure to conform to more secular and liberal norms can create a rift between one's spirituality and social participation. However, standing firm in one's convictions — guided by tact and respect — upholds the dignity of one's beliefs while fostering meaningful discussions and relationships. It is the consistently lived-out expression of faith that often speaks louder than any sermon could.

Considering the current socio-political climate, Christians must be adept at translating their values into actionable public policies and community development best practices. **This transition from the personal to the political, from the private to the public, should enhance, not compromise, the integrity of individual faith**. It offers an opportunity to advocate for policies that reinforce the protection of religious freedoms, the sanctity of life, traditional family values, and care for the marginalized, anchoring societal structures in moral principles.

In the entrepreneurial realm, integrating faith with business involves much more than financial success; it's about shaping an enterprise that embodies Christian ethics through fair practices, equitable treatment of employees, and social responsibility. This perspective turns a profession into a vocation, imbuing work with purpose, service and mission. For Christian entrepreneurs and business owners, business is an avenue to demonstrate how the market can serve people, reflecting the kingdom values of stewardship and care for one's neighbor.

As the contours of a Jesus-above-all identity in society take shape, an enriched sense of purpose emerges. The pursuit of authenticity is not a solitary endeavor but a collective journey — a tapestry woven from individual threads of conviction, influencing the world around you.

Living Authentically through Community Engagement

For the Christian individual, navigating the complexities of society while maintaining faith-based integrity is paramount. In today's web of social interactions, it becomes increasingly crucial to infuse Christian values seamlessly into community engagement. Achieving this begins with intentional living — making conscious decisions that reflect Christian moral teachings in all corners of public life. Whether deciding how to vote, what causes to support, or even how to address conflict in the workplace, each choice should align with one's spiritual convictions.

The Power of Gentle Witness

One effective strategy is embracing the role of a gentle witness in daily life. This approach centers on embodying Christian principles rather than merely advocating for them. For example, choosing to exhibit love, patience, and kindness in interactions signals a commitment to Christian values more powerfully than words alone could ever convey. This form of silent testimony can profoundly influence others and offer a clear picture of what faith in action looks like.

Fostering Dialogue and Understanding

Engaging in respectful dialogue with others, particularly those who hold differing views, is another vital element. Such discourse is not about proving a point but rather demonstrating the grace and humility that one's faith espouses. When contributing to community efforts or participating in civic duties, **the goal is to build bridges of understanding, rather than creating divisions**. By listening earnestly and speaking with compassion, one can foster an atmosphere conducive to shared growth and harmony.

Service as a Pathway

The Christian call to service provides yet another avenue for integrating faith into social engagement. Volunteering and community service resonate with the Christian imperative to care for the least among us, while also providing the opportunity to witness to those who do not know about Jesus Christ and His love for them. Through service, the abstract concept of love becomes a tangible act, reinforcing the spiritual mission within diverse community contexts. It is the physical manifestation of faith — a clear sign that one's beliefs are not confined to the private realm but are active and influential in the wider world.

Ethical Stewardship in the Marketplace

In the marketplace, Christian ethics guides business practices, such as transparency and fairness, which engender trust and respect. If you're an entrepreneur, incorporating principles of fair treatment and fiscal responsibility can set a powerful example. For those navigating their professional careers, seeking justice and integrity in the workplace underscores a commitment to Christian values, which can inspire colleagues and industry peers alike.

Advocacy Rooted in Faith

Raising one's voice for policies and initiatives that align with Christian teachings is another practical way to weave faith into the fabric of civic life. Advocating for religious freedom, protecting the marginalized, and championing the sanctity of life are all actions that can support Scripture. By doing so, one not only takes a stand for personal beliefs but also contributes to the moral advancement of society at large.

Nurturing Personal and Collective Growth

It is important to invest in personal spiritual growth as well as collective progress. Joining or forming faith-based groups dedicated to discussing and addressing social issues through a Biblical lens can be a catalyst for both. Sharing experiences, exploring Biblical teachings, and collectively seeking wisdom provides a firmer foundation for integrating faith and social engagement in a way that edifies both the individual and the community.

The Watchful Eye of Integrity

In the pursuit of aligning one's faith with their actions in society, an unwavering commitment to integrity proves indispensable. **Integrity demands that we conduct ourselves with the same virtues in public as we do in private.** It acts as the bridging force between personal beliefs and social conduct, ensuring that one does not contradict the other. Yet the practical maintenance of integrity is an ongoing endeavor, one that calls for constant self-assessment and conscious alignment with our moral compass. Consider the Biblical admonition found in Proverbs 11:3, *"The integrity of the upright guides them, but the unfaithful are destroyed by their duplicity."* This ancient wisdom serves as a stark reminder of the protective and guiding power of integrity in our lives.

Authenticity in the Face of Adversity

To live authentically is to understand that your spiritual journey is not separate from the rest of your existence. **When circumstances challenge your values, respond with authenticity, rather than retreat or compromise.** Let the beatitudes be your blueprint in business dealings, community relations, and even in the voting booth. By doing so, you'll find that the social structures and systems you engage with will not only test but also strengthen your faith. **Resilience in the face of adversity doesn't only build character but also fosters a sense of inner peace, knowing that your external actions are congruent with your spiritual beliefs.**

Continuous Self-improvement

Maintaining integrity is not a static achievement but a dynamic process of self-improvement and growth. It involves not resting on past moral victories but striving for new heights in character development. A practical step is regular self-reflection, which offers the opportunity to assess whether your actions align with your professed beliefs. These moments of reflection should be coupled with prayer and meditation, calling upon divine wisdom for guidance.

You can also consider having an accountability partner or become part of a small discipleship group, where each like-minded member helps support the other in his or her walk to become more like Jesus.

The Bible teaches us to *"carry each other's burdens"* (Galatians 6:2), and in doing so, our own load becomes lighter. Therefore, create a community of support that holds you accountable, and reciprocate by being a pillar of support for others.

Transparent Communication

Open and honest communication underscores the integrity of our interactions. Whether it's in personal conversations or professional collaborations, being transparent about your motivations, decisions, wins / losses, and future commitments prevents misunderstandings and builds trust. Ensure that your word is your bond, and do not make promises you cannot keep. **Speak the truth in love** (Ephesians 4:15), remembering that transparency does not necessitate harshness but can be exercised with grace and respect.

The Harmony of Work and Worship

In our careers and ventures, it is vital to **remember that our work can be an act of worship**. As we seek to integrate our faith into every aspect of our lives, our occupations should not be exceptions. Viewing your professional aspirations through the lens of stewardship and service elevates the mundane to the miraculous and transforms your daily tasks into opportunities for spiritual fulfillment. The simple act of excellence in one's field can be a powerful testimony of the values we hold dear.

Embrace Lifelong Learning

A well-rounded understanding of the world enhances our ability to live integrated lives. By embracing learning—whether through theology, politics, or economics—we equip ourselves with the critical tools to engage society effectively. Staying informed and open to new insights allows us to navigate complex social terrains without compromising our spiritual integrity. Gaining knowledge should be seen as an act of empowerment that aids us in aligning our spiritual walk with our societal impact.

Navigating Ethical Dilemmas

Ethical dilemmas will naturally arise as we juggle different roles and responsibilities. Approaching these crossroads requires discernment and the courage to make decisions that may not be popular but are right. It's at these junctures that **prayerful consideration and counsel from trusted advisors become invaluable**. Remember, your choice in difficult circumstances speaks volumes about your character and stands as a witness to the values you espouse as an ambassador for Christ (2 Corinthians 5:20).

Enacting Change with Conviction

Let us then move forward with conviction, resolute in harmonizing our spiritual beliefs with our societal engagement. May we successfully navigate the path that bears witness to our deepest convictions, acting with courage and clarity.

Remember, in this pursuit, authenticity is not the destination but a manner of traveling. It is in the daily decisions, the conversations we engage in, and the relationships we build that our true testament as believers becomes evident. Let us tread this path with unwavering faith, vigilant in aligning our actions with the Biblical truth that anchors us.

WHEN FAITH FEELS LIKE FRICTION

In the quiet stir of early evening, at the juncture of another strenuous work day's end and the sanctuary of twilight repose, Michael found himself wrestling once more with the invisible threads that seemed to stitch together his faith and his roots. Feet planted in the soft earth of his mother's garden, the smell of fertile soil hung heavy in the air, spiced with the faintest hint of jasmine. He was in the midst of uprooting weeds, the unruly invaders of his mother's prized carrots, when the conflict in his soul felt akin to the stubborn roots he tugged at.

The garden, a patchwork quilt of vibrant greens and muted colors, encircled by the weathered wooden fence, served as a haven, not only for his mother's vegetables but also for his roiling thoughts. As the equinox sun dipped low, casting honey-gold beams across the foliage, Michael's mind wandered to the stark white walls of the local church, standing at odds with the rich, dark faces that filled its pews. Here, he found refuge in scriptures that spoke of love, discipline, and unwavering conservative values that often seemed out of step with the pulsing heartbeat of his community's drums of progress and change.

Surrounded by peers who marveled at his devout worship, yet frequently misunderstood his more conservative stance, Michael knew all too well the tightrope he walked. Each Sunday sermon was followed by lively debates at the family lunch table, where perspectives often clashed like cymbals, resounding in his ears long after the dishes were cleared. His Aunt Tessa, a spirited advocate for social reform, would lean across the heirloom tablecloth, her voice soft yet insistent, questioning how he could espouse beliefs that seemed to her a relic of times past.

Just last week, seeking counsel, Michael had turned to the story of Amos, a man of God and of justice, whose strides through ancient streets spoke of balancing righteousness with the call for societal transformation. The tale had filled the room like ancient incense, a narrative of inspiration and conviction that cloaked him with an understanding that it was indeed possible to uphold one's faith while embracing their heritage.

As he dug around another obstinate weed, though, the doubts seeped back in. Michael reflected on the day he'd stood before young minds as a guest speaker at his alma mater. Their expectant eyes had questioned whether his adherence to tradition left room for their futuristic aspirations. His address had depicted an intricate dance of ideologies, painting a picture of harmony achievable through mutual respect and understanding, the words echoing those of Paul in Corinth - a testament to a timeless struggle for alignment between personal convictions and communal ties.

The church's steeple, visible just over the fence line, was a beacon against the sky now bruised with purples and blues as night began to descend. The tensions within Michael whispered like the leaves in the evening zephyr, and a silent prayer passed his lips as he considered the daily lives of those who shared his struggle. To what extent can the cultivation of one's spiritual garden sow seeds of accord within the tapestry of a historically collective culture? Such was the question that hummed through Michael's mind as the jasmine scent grew bolder, an answer as yet unfound, as evanescent as the twilight itself.

The Crossroads of Conviction and Culture

At the intersection of faith and cultural identity, Black Christians with conservative views can find themselves navigating a complex terrain of beliefs and community expectations. African American history is woven with threads of faith and collective progress, yet for some, the texture of this tapestry changes when Christianity and conservatism enter the picture. Understanding the roots of internal community tension for those at this crossroads is not just about excavating historical challenges, but it is also about acknowledging the ever-evolving dynamics of spirituality and cultural affinity.

The path to harmonizing faith-based beliefs with cultural community traditions is akin to traversing a labyrinth; it requires patience, wisdom, and a clear-eyed recognition of both spiritual and social landscapes. Biblical teachings, which serve as the bedrock of conservative Christian values, often emphasize principles that can be at odds with the prevailing winds of social and political ideologies that equally shape the Black experience. Recognizing this dichotomy sets the stage for a nuanced discussion about coherence in the life of a believer who stands firmly within these two worlds.

Navigating the coexistence of faith and culture is not about compromise; it is about the pursuit of authenticity in one's beliefs and actions. **It is also about the courage to stand alone when neces-**

sary, fortified by spiritual conviction, while striving to remain an integral part of a community whose historical journey is marked by unity and resilience. The challenge is assertive but not indomitable: How does one honor the legacy of collective progress without surrendering core religious values?

Anecdotes and case studies from those who have walked this path before offer both solace and strategy. They show how balancing faith and cultural identity can not only be done but done well, leading to enriched lives and stronger communities. These stories are not just narratives of survival but testimonies to the power of living one's truth amidst a diversity of beliefs.

Each believer's journey is deeply personal, yet it unfolds within the broader expanse of a community's narrative. The witness of those who reconcile their conservative Christian faith with their cultural identity provides invaluable lessons. Their experiences reveal the importance of dialogue, the strength found in diversity, and the significance of roots that anchor us through the storm of societal change.

It is in the engagement with this tension – rather than the evasion of it – that we find growth, understanding, and unexpected common ground. For the individual whose beliefs can feel like friction against the grain of community norms, **the invitation is to embrace this tension as a catalyst for dialogue rather than a chasm to avoid.**

Solidarity and spirituality need not be at odds. By steadfastly navigating conservatism within the Black Christian journey, the faithful can forge a path that honors both their heritage and their spiritual convictions – without losing sight of the community's broader objectives. This balance calls for wisdom, grace, and an unwavering commitment to one's principles, all undergirded by the redemptive love that is central to the Christian faith. It is here, in the junction of conviction and compassion, that a transformative way forward emerges, one conversation, one action, one prayer at a time.

Understanding cultural context is pivotal when exploring the unique position of Black Christians who uphold conservative views. Historically, the Black Church has been a cornerstone for community and civil rights advocacy. This powerful legacy often aligns with more liberal perspectives on social justice, creating a default expectation among many within the Black community. As a result, Black Christians with conservative beliefs can find themselves in a challenging place, holding values that diverge from these community norms.

However, faith-based conservatism isn't monolithic, and it certainly isn't synonymous with racial insensitivity or ignorance of social issues. Conservative Black Christians often advocate for policies that support family structure, economic empowerment, and educational choice — areas deeply relevant to the Black community's advancement. In essence, their conservative stance is rooted in a desire for community growth, albeit through a different ideological lens. **It's vital for these individuals to recognize that their conservative values do not betray their cultural identity but represent another pathway to community upliftment.**

For Black Christians navigating this delicate juncture, it may feel like treading a line between historical heritage and personal conviction. This internal struggle can evoke feelings of isolation, misunderstanding or condemnation from both within the black church community and the broader cultural context. Yet, it is crucial to discern that cultural progression isn't owned by any single political ideology. Jesus himself presented radical ideas that were often at odds with the prevailing norms of his time. Following His example, it is possible to pursue a conservative approach to problem-solving while also advocating for positive change in society.

Biblical precedence backs the idea of principled dissent. The Scriptures are replete with examples of individuals who stood firmly against the tide, not out of contrarian pride but guided by divine wisdom. In a similar vein, Black Christians with conservative views can take solace in the biblical assurance that standing firm in one's convictions is not just admirable but is an act of spiritual obedience. Their faith can be the anchor, allowing them to weather the friction of differing community perspectives while remaining true to both their cultural heritage and personal beliefs.

Respecting traditions doesn't necessarily mean adhering to them when they conflict with one's religious principles. It's about engaging in meaningful dialogue, fostering understanding, and creating spaces where diverse viewpoints within the Black community are not just tolerated but welcomed and encouraged. Integrating conservative principles with social progress can offer comprehensive solutions that might be overlooked if only mainstream ideologies are considered.

Leveraging personal experiences, sharing stories of resilience and success can significantly impact the perception of conservatism within the community. Real-world examples serve as tangible evidence that conservative beliefs can coincide with cultural progress and social responsibility. By articulating how conservative policies can lead to positive change for individuals, families and communities alike, the perceived gap between faith and cultural identity begins to close.

Empowerment through education is also crucial as it equips individuals with the knowledge to make informed political decisions that align with their core values. Understanding the historical and theological underpinnings of conservative philosophy enables one to articulate and defend their position with confidence and grace.

Moreover, the collective power of a supportive community should not be underestimated. **Building networks of like-minded individuals can provide a sense of belonging and encouragement, fostering a germination ground for conservative ideas to be shared and embraced within Christian circles.** Establishing forums for open conversation allows for the exchange of ideas and mutual edification — **key for those who find themselves as minorities within the minority**.

As we delve deeper into navigating this complex interplay between faith-based beliefs and cultural traditions, remember that internal tension can be a catalyst for growth and clarity. It's through this friction that one can vigorously examine personal faith, wrestle with difficult questions, and emerge with a more fortified sense of identity – emboldened to contribute to the community in a manner that is both respectful and authentic.

Navigating the Intersection of Faith and Culture

Navigating the coexistence of faith-based beliefs with cultural community traditions is no small feat. **For Black Christians with conservative views, this path can seem like walking a delicate tightrope, with each step needing to be measured and intentional.** It is important to approach such a path with a spirit of understanding and respect for both your faith and your cultural heritage. The key is not to see these two aspects of your identity as mutually exclusive but to find the intersections where they can enrich each other. Often, this requires a deep reflection on the core values that define your spirituality and how these can be harmoniously aligned with the cultural norms and expectations that are important within the Black community.

Embracing your Christian conservative values does not mean you must reject the cultural traditions that have been a bedrock for the community. It is crucial to appreciate the historical context and significance of these traditions, understanding the role they have played in the journey towards equality and collective progress. At the same time, your faith may lead you to different conclusions on certain social or political issues. Here, frank yet respectful conversations can bridge the gap. **Engaging with community leaders, elders, and peers in a dialogue about your faith-based beliefs creates opportunities to shed light on your perspective and listen to theirs, promoting mutual understanding.**

Moreover, finding fellowship with those who share your views can be a deep well of support. There are likely others within the community who also hold conservative Christian views, and connecting with them can offer solace and strength. **This fellowship does not act to segregate but to fortify the individual so that they can engage more confidently with the broader community without feeling isolated in their beliefs.** To facilitate this, it would be beneficial to seek out or even establish groups – whether within your church or in other communal spaces with Christians of different races – that provide this affinity and understanding.

In the realm of practical application, your conservative Christian principles can inform your decision-making processes in various aspects of life. Whether it's in business, where your moral compass can guide ethical practices, or in community service, where your faith can inspire a compassionate approach to leadership. **Implementing these principles should be done with humility and respect for others' viewpoints, showing that your choices are not about imposing beliefs but living by the convictions that define you.**

Reflecting on scriptural teachings, the principle of "love thy neighbor" is widely emphasized. This can be a foundational guide in all interactions, ensuring that even when disagreements arise, they are handled with kindness and patience. **It's also worth remembering that Jesus Christ himself navigated a diverse array of cultures and customs, engaging with people from all walks of life without compromising His message. His example serves as a powerful blueprint for modern believers on how to maintain Biblical integrity while building bridges across various cultural divides.**

Finding inspiration in the lives of past and present Christian leaders who have dealt with similar situations can be immensely helpful. Many have written about or spoken on how they managed to reconcile their conservative beliefs with their cultural identities. These case studies can provide practical steps and encouragement as you chart your own course.

When bringing your faith into public discourse it is crucial to do so with grace and eloquence. This involves framing your arguments in a way that is understandable and relatable, and avoiding conflict by steering clear of antagonistic rhetoric. Your voice is most powerful when it resonates with compassion and wisdom, and less so with judgment or divisiveness.

In truth, your journey is about more than just balancing different aspects of your identity; it's about living out your convictions with authenticity. Although friction might arise, when handled with savvy and sensitivity, it can lead to growth for both you and your community. Through this process, **you are tasked with forging a path that celebrates the totality of who you are, the faith you uphold, and the cultural ties that bind you to both believers and unbelievers that share a rich historical legacy.** Remember, friction can be transformative, and with each challenge comes the opportunity to demonstrate the inclusive and enduring nature of your faith.

Faith-Cultural Equilibrium Model

Historical Context

Understanding the delicate balance between faith-based beliefs and cultural community traditions begins with an exploration of the historical tapestry that weaves together the Black Christian experience. Historically, Black Christians have been at the forefront of major social movements, advocating for civil rights and justice while upholding their conservative values. Key figures such as Frederick Douglass, Booker T. Washington and Dr. Martin Luther King Jr. navigated their advocacy within a conservative and Christian framework, emphasizing moral rectitude and personal responsibility alongside their pursuit for social equality. Reflecting on their legacies reveals the tenacious grip that faith had in steering their ideologies and actions - despite societal pressures that often ran counter to their conservative beliefs.

Cultural Influences

The social fabric of the Black community is rich with traditions and values that have been passed down through generations. This cultural foundation often promotes a collective identity that emphasizes unity and progress. Yet within this collective aspiration resides a diverse spectrum of thought, where conservative views can both complement and clash with the broader narrative. Cultural traditions, such as strong family ties and community support systems, often align well with conservative principles, reinforcing the importance of societal structures and shared responsibilities.

Theological Perspective

At the heart of the friction between faith and black culture is a divergent interpretation of theological teachings. The Black Christian conservative often looks to scripture and doctrine as the ultimate guide for their principles, challenging secular trends that may conflict with their religious convictions. Scripture provides not a backdrop but a blueprint for living, influencing perspectives on key issues like marriage, sanctity of life, and personal integrity. It is through the lens of their faith that conservative Black Christians evaluate their cultural experiences and make decisions that reflect their commitment to their spiritual journey.

Social and Political Impact

Conservative values invariably make their way into the broader discourse on social and political issues. Black Christians with conservative views might find themselves advocating for policies that prioritize family stability, school choice, or welfare reform - issues that transcend racial lines yet can be contentious within the black community. The interplay between these values and the community's call for social justice presents an arena where faith principles must be both stalwart and fluid, adaptable to the shifting landscapes of social needs and political debates.

The practical application of this Faith-Culture Equilibrium Model framework involves a navigation that is both discerning and diplomatic. By understanding the historical underpinnings, cultural bearings, and theological foundations of their conservative stance, Black Christians can engage more confidently and constructively with their communities.

A case study that illustrates the positive outcomes of this dynamic balance can be seen in the life of a community leader who integrates their conservative Christian views with a commitment to social entrepreneurship. By establishing programs that promote financial literacy and entrepreneurship, they address economic disparities while adhering to their belief in self-reliance and the dignity of work. Their initiatives create avenues for dialogue and progress within the community, demonstrating the compatibility of conservative values with the advancement of community goals.

Another example is found in the realm of education, where Black Christian conservatives champion school choice initiatives, acknowledging the legacy of inequity, unacceptable results and the widespread lack of rigor in public education while advocating for the freedom of parents to choose the best educational setting for their children, whether it involves private schools, parochial schools, or even charter schools. This approach respects the cultural emphasis on the value of education within the Black community while upholding the conservative principle of individual liberty.

In summary, the Faith-Cultural Equilibrium Model is not a rigid construct but a humble yet potentially dynamic framework that guides individuals in harmonizing their deeply held beliefs with their cultural identity. It underscores the importance of context - historical, cultural, theological, and social - in shaping the contours of conservative thought within the Black Christian experience. By engaging with each component of the model, individuals can navigate the terrain of community expectations and faith principles with both conviction and cultural sensitivity. The model offers a blueprint for fostering an authentic and impactful life that honors one's spiritual and communal heritage.

Navigate the Coexistence of Faith and Culture

Blending faith-based beliefs with cultural community traditions is an art of delicate balance, one that requires both conviction and compassion. The key to mastering this balance lies in respecting the rich cultural traditions while staying true to the core of our conservative Christian values. We are encouraged to *"let love be genuine. Abhor what is evil; hold fast to what is good"* (Romans 12:9), thus maintaining our integrity even as we actively engage in the cultural sphere that may contain both sacred and secular influences.

As individuals navigate these troubled waters, practical steps can foster this tricky coexistence. Establishing open dialogues, initiating community mentorship programs, and engaging in collaborative initiatives serve as tangible examples. These approaches strengthen ties and encourage mutual understanding, leading to a healthier synthesis of belief and tradition. Engage honestly with your community, build upon shared values, and stand firm in your convictions.

Let us take these lessons and build bridges where there once were walls, ensuring that our faith not only anchors us but also allows us to embrace others within our community. With the Lord's guidance and a heartfelt commitment to our shared human experience, we can turn friction into forward momentum, creating a unified and thriving community that honors both our conservative values and our rich cultural heritage.

THE MYTH OF INDIFFERENCE: CHRISTIAN CONSERVATISM AND SOCIAL JUSTICE

The air was crisp, with a scent of pine lingering on a gentle breeze. In a small, timber-framed church nestled in the bosom of an old forest, Reverend Carpenter stood outside the entrance, a Bible clutched in one hand, his gaze tracing the horizon where the forest gave way to the town of Providence. The townfolk had dismissed the evening's sermon as mere tradition; their lives were driven by needs less ephemeral, more economic.

Often, they had labeled John as a figure untouched by the world's grime, with his sturdy beliefs about Christian conservatism. They said he lived in a spiritual haven, divorced from the struggles of the present age. Yet, as he closed his eyes to the setting sun, a sense of disquiet lodged itself within his chest, like a chunk of timber refusing to burn.

John recalled the dialogue that had stirred earlier that day in the fellowship hall, where he ventured in hopes of discussing the new housing project for the less fortunate. "Reverend," they had said, "your heart's in the right place, but your approach is out of touch." He remembered the warmth of the hall, the smell of varnish on the wooden benches, and the clanking of construction outside – a resounding metaphor for the change he wished to bring forth.

Opening his Bible to the book of Micah, John whispered along with the winds, "*Do justice, love kindness, walk humbly with your God.*" These ancient words fuelled him, not with a clinging to tradition, but with a call to action deeply rooted in faith. His approach to social justice wasn't hinged on the turn of a blind eye, but rather on the profound belief that change must spring from moral conviction, a conservative value often misunderstood by those who wore their liberalism like a badge of honor.

As dusk beckoned the stars into view, John interacted with the environment of his church – the polished oak pews, the altar where the cross cast a long shadow on the wall, the smell of wax from candles long extinguished. He mulled over the hunger he saw in the eyes of children as he served them at the town's soup kitchen, not just for the meal, but for the fulfillment of a love as tangible as bread and as satisfying as warmth in winter.

There, in the womb of the church, under the watchful eyes of the stained-glass saints, John crafted a message of togetherness in this world of scattered allegiances. His thoughts paved the way for a sermon that might bridge the divide: in Christ's teaching was the embodiment of conservative values that were not blind to suffering, but rather deeply engaged in the alleviation of it. His conservatism, he felt, was the very vessel for compassion, a truth regrettably lost in translation.

The chime of the clock tower in the heart of Providence rang, marking the passage of another hour. John considered how his own faith, through the prism of scriptures and the lens of conservatism, could become a beacon of practical help and hope. Could the stalwarts of progress recognize the depth of commitment to justice that lay in his philosophy of conservatism? What depths of understanding and unity could we reach if we listened to the rhythms of each other's hearts?

Unraveling the Paradox: A Conservative Call to Justice

Christian conservatism within the Black community often conjures images of staunch, unyielding adherence to tradition, potentially at the expense of progressive social movements. However, this view neglects the intricate tapestry of spiritual conviction and social conscience that defines a vast majority of Black Christian conservatives. Far from being disengaged or indifferent, many within this ideological fold find themselves deeply intertwined with the pursuits of justice and equality, guided by time-honored scriptural principles that affirm their commitment to societal welfare. Herein lies the paradox that this chapter seeks to demystify; the perceived ideological chasm between Christian conservatism and social justice is bridged by a biblical framework that advocates for both righteousness and compassion in equal measure.

The myths that have long circulated about Christian conservatism's apparent apathy towards social issues are confronted head-on as we delve into the rich Biblical tradition that informs the conservative perspective on justice. Scripture is replete with calls to *"do justice, love mercy, and walk humbly with God"* (Micah 6:8), laying the foundational ethos for Christians to engage actively with the world's inequities. Far from evading the demands of social justice, the conservative approach seeks to address these yearnings through a prism of divine instruction, promoting the welfare of the community without compromising scriptural integrity.

A critical exploration of this biblical view on justice brings to light its relevance in addressing modern social issues. From economic disparity to racial tensions, Christian conservatism gravitates towards sustainable and spiritually aligned solutions. In Jesus' own ministry, one witnesses a balance between upholding moral absolutes and embracing those marginalized by the societal norms of the time — offering a pattern for present-day believers striving to harmonize their conservative beliefs with a heart for justice.

The exposition not only contrasts Christian conservative approaches to social justice with other ideological frameworks but also champions the unique contributions this worldview brings to public discourse. From the emphasis on personal responsibility to the advocacy for strong family units, the conservative lens often promotes social structures that aim to empower rather than enable, that foster self-sufficiency in conjunction with a supportive community.

There is a pervasive narrative that paints Christian conservatism with a broad brush of indifference when it comes to matters of social justice. Yet, such a portrayal is not only reductionist but fundamentally mistaken. At the same time, to be candid, the word "social justice" does not have a clear definition today, for it can mean different things for different people, thus further complicating how to go about caring for the needy, the orphaned, the underprivileged, and the widowed, whether in the name of "social justice" or something else. At the heart of Christian conservative beliefs is an enduring concern for societal well being grounded in scriptural truths. This commitment to caring for others is not passive; it is a dynamic, action-oriented ethos that prioritizes the inherent dignity of every individual as created in the image of God.

Truth be told, Christian conservatives engage with social justice very differently from secular viewpoints. They adhere to a biblical framework that offers not just temporal aids or how-to practical advice but seeks to transform lives through the spreading of the Gospel of Jesus Christ. The conservative approach to justice focuses on upholding moral absolutes, righteousness and individual responsibility, considering these as the bedrocks for any lasting social change. For conservatives, the measure of justice does not revolve around monetary redistribution, funding wars on poverty and systemic racism, or extravagant government programs that put America further in debt — it seeks to care for the heart and soul of each person, as well as his or her physical needs.

This deep-rooted concern for justice, paired with an emphasis on charity, finds expression in numerous practical ways. Take, for instance, the extensive network of church-based programs that provide everything from food and shelter to education and job training. These initiatives are built on the conviction that assisting our neighbor is not merely a civic duty but an integral facet of Christian faith. It's these faith-driven actions, quietly carried out by countless believers, that embody a sincere commitment to resolving the knotty challenges of inequality and need. **One key question to look into the Bible for an answer: when it comes to justice and caring for the less fortunate, is that responsibility more for the individual believer to uphold or is it the primary responsibility of the government?**

Unfortunately, the conservative Christian's vision of social justice is not always echoed in mainstream media or social conversations. Instead of recognition, there's often unfounded skepticism regarding their intentions or impact. Yet by examining the lives and contributions of Christian conservative individuals and communities, we reveal a living tapestry of care and service that belies the myth of indifference. Stories abound of people and organizations, oftentimes anonymous or with little-to-no recognition or acclaim, that have stood in the gap for the marginalized, driven by faith and not a desire for acknowledgment.

Looking beyond these acts of service, Christian conservatives propose policies and perspectives informed by a holistic view of humanity. The focus is on fostering environments where personal responsibility is encouraged, and the sanctity of the family unit is revered — as these are seen as vital elements to societal prosperity.

To underscore how important the individual and family unit are to our society, I share one of the greatest lessons I learned from one of my spiritual mentors, Dr. Tony Evans, on the value of having strong families led by strong individuals, particularly strong and present fathers. If we do not have strong and loving fathers in the homes leading strong families, those families will inevitably impact how strong our churches will be, and those churches will then have a say in how strong our communities will be, and those communities will consequently impact how strong our cities will be, and those cities will subsequently impact how strong our counties will be, and those counties will undoubtedly impact how strong our states will be, and those states will absolutely impact how strong our country will be, and the type of country America will be will absolutely have an impact on the type of world we will live in.

Thus, if you want a better world, a better America, better states, better counties, better cities, better communities, better churches, and better families, it starts by the people raising the family, which absolutely includes having better men present to help raise the family in a Godly manner, thus why the

nationwide crisis of fatherlessness to the Black community is so important from both a community and spiritual perspective.

It is without question that Satan wants to break up our homes and our families, and one of the best ways to do that is to take the fathers out of the homes by any means - or policies - necessary. All Christians, conservative or otherwise, in the Black community, as well as across all races, should come together and target the vast reduction of fatherlessness in the homes of our families as one of its top community priorities in the name of social justice.

In contrast to the sweeping generalizations about their supposed apathy towards social issues, Christian conservatives are actively proposing and participating in solutions that they believe align with enduring truths. These solutions, however, might not always align with the contemporary social justice lexicon, which is why dialogue and understanding are crucial. They advocate for a brand of justice that not only provides for the physical needs but also dignifies individuals by empowering them to rise above their circumstances to get back on their feet and not become overly dependent on government subsistence.

It's important to discern the cornerstone upon which Christian conservative social justice rests: love and respect for the intrinsic worth of every human soul made in the image of God. The response to injustice is, therefore, not rooted in a political ideology but in a divine command to love one's neighbor as oneself, one of the two Great Commandments that Jesus gave us in Matthew 22:36-40. This powerful motivator has, throughout history, compelled believers to acts of great compassion and advocacy. From the abolition of slavery to modern-day efforts against human trafficking, Christian conservatives have been at the forefront, often unsung and overlooked, in the quest for justice and human dignity.

Tackling Tough Questions: A Biblical Perspective on Social Issues

The Scriptural Perspective on Justice

At the heart of Christian conservatism is an unwavering commitment to scriptural authority. The Bible is replete with exhortations to pursue justice, and throughout its metanarrative, justice is inextricably linked not just to punishment or retribution, but to righteousness, equality, and mercy. For instance, the biblical prophets, from Amos to Isaiah, did not shy away from denouncing exploitation and calling for justice to *"roll on like a river, righteousness like a never-failing stream!"* (Amos 5:24). Their bold declarations remind us that engaging with social issues is not a novel concept but a fundamental aspect of our spiritual heritage. It is not a matter of whether one should pursue justice, but more so on how to best pursue justice.

Bridging Faith and Works

One cannot discuss Christian perspectives on social justice without addressing the delicate balance between faith and works, which James 2:26 so eloquently encapsulates: *"Faith without works is dead."* This verse admonishes believers that their faith is demonstrated and authenticated by their actions. Therefore, **it is not enough to merely profess concern for the disenfranchised; the Biblical mandate is to be the hands and feet of Jesus in a world rife with in-**

equality and suffering. Christian conservatism supports this holistic approach to faith, one that goes beyond the pews and into the community.

The Parable of the Good Samaritan: Lessons in Social Responsibility

The Parable of the Good Samaritan (Luke 10:25-37) is a powerful teaching moment that underscores the virtue of neighborly love, crossing societal boundaries. This narrative is a rallying call to action, encouraging the faithful not to pass by on the other side of the road, but to be moved by compassion and to help those in dire straits, even if the person needing help is different from you. While some may interpret Christian conservatism as insular, this parable reveals the expansive heart of biblical justice, which calls us to care for even those who are outside our immediate circles.

Economics and Generosity in Biblical Teachings

A robust understanding of the biblical perspective on justice must also engage with economic aspects. Scripture advises fair treatment in business (Leviticus 19:35-36) and advocates for the provision for the poor, such as leaving gleanings of harvest for those in need (Leviticus 19:9-10). Acts of giving and generosity are not just suggested; they are held up as evidence of a transformed heart. Consequently, Christian conservatism recognizes fiscal responsibility both as a personal virtue and a means to facilitate broader social justice through generosity.

The Sanctity of Life and Family Values

Fundamental to the Christian conservative ethos is the sanctity of life and the importance of traditional family values. **These stances are not merely political positions but extensions of biblical principles that honor life at all stages (Psalm 139:13-16) and uphold the family as a fundamental unit of society (Ephesians 5:22-6:4).** The commitment to these principles drives significant community involvement and advocacy for policies that support the well-being of families and the protection of the vulnerable.

Integrating Faith in Policy Advocacy

Christian conservatives are often actively involved in policy advocacy, driven by a desire to see biblical ideals reflected in the laws of the land. Whether it is fighting against injustices such as human trafficking or championing religious liberty, the intent is to influence society in ways that are consistent with Christian values. This active participation demonstrates a deep engagement with social issues contrary to the allegations of indifference.

Faith in Action: Serving the Marginalized

The Bible is clear about the imperative to serve the marginalized; Proverbs 31:8-9 calls us to *"Speak up for those who cannot speak for themselves, for the rights of all who are destitute."* Christian conservatives take this mandate to heart, supporting and initiating numerous outreach programs, from foster care to prison ministries. By embodying this ethic of service, they refute the myth of inaction and boldly express their faith's convictions in tangible and transformative ways.

The faith-based approach to social justice is richly informed by biblical teachings and fueled by a desire to manifest faith through action. This commitment often translates into a life of individual service, advocacy, and generosity that engages the social fabric of communities, thus demonstrating a profound dedication to fostering just and more equitable societies.

Christian conservatism, often seen as at odds with social justice, actually holds unique approaches that echo with profound spiritual and moral underpinnings. **Contrary to some ideologies which may rely primarily on significant government intervention and policies as mechanisms for social change, Christian conservative philosophy tends to promote individual morality, economic empowerment and community-based initiatives as the bedrock for justice and equality.** This perspective is far from being indifferent; instead, it suggests a different path to achieving societal well-being — one that is closely aligned with personal responsibility and Biblical values.

The Christian conservative views on justice are deeply rooted in the Biblical mandate to 'love thy neighbor.' This commandment pushes believers to engage in acts that directly support and uplift others. **Unlike some secular approaches to social justice, which might prioritize systemic change to improve individual circumstances, a Christian conservative approach often advocates for direct personal involvement and grassroots activism as means to manifest God's love and justice in the world.** This might include mentoring young people, supporting local businesses, upskilling underrepresented populations in technology and trades in demand, and contributing to charitable causes.

Divergence in Dependencies

There's also a divergence in dependence. **Where some ideologies lean heavily on the state to provide solutions to social issues, Christian conservatism calls for limited government intervention, encouraging a society where individuals, families and faith-based organizations play a significant role in social welfare.** It is believed that overreliance on government can sometimes inadvertently disempower individuals and their communities, leaving local knowledge and compassion underutilized. Instead, initiatives driven by individuals and community leaders are seen as more adaptable and personally invested in the wellness of their constituents.

Frameworks of Responsibility

The frames of responsibility also differ significantly. The conservative Christian tradition emphasizes personal accountability — not only to God but to one's community. This approach encourages people to live virtuous lives and make choices that reflect the collective morality taught by Scripture. **Other more liberal ideologies might focus more on collective rights and societal responsibilities, promoting the idea that it is primarily institutions and structures that must change to facilitate individual transformation. In contrast, the Christian conservative believes transformation begins within the individual, rippling out to affect societal change.**

Sustainable Altruism

When it comes to philanthropy and aid, Christian conservatism stresses sustainable support over temporary band-aid fixes. Charity and development efforts are geared toward enabling individuals to help themselves in the long run rather than providing a one-time aid that does not contribute to lasting change. This is based on the belief that dignity comes from the ability to be self-sufficient, mirroring the proverb of teaching one to fish rather than simply giving a fish. Other social justice approaches may advocate for immediate and widespread wealth redistribution as a solution to poverty, which contrasts with the empowerment-based philanthropy championed by many Christian conservatives.

Ethical Imperatives

Ethics play an enormous role in Christian conservative philosophy; **it's not simply about alleviating the symptoms of injustice but also addressing the moral roots that may contribute to it. Whereas some ideologies might focus exclusively on outcomes such as inequality, the Christian conservative perspective also explores root causes like lack of strong work ethic, corruption, and moral decay.** Addressing these moral undercurrents is seen as essential to cultivating a just and honorable society.

Solidarity and Compassion

One should not misconstrue this as a lack of compassion for those who suffer under systemic oppression. Many Christian conservatives deeply understand injustice and seek to confront it in ways that align with their faith. They often advocate for policies and practices that they believe will have long-term benefits over those that provide immediate, but perhaps unsustainable relief. They wage battle against poverty and injustice not through revamping systems alone but through nurturing changed hearts and renewed minds, aiming for a community where justice rolls down like a river, informed by faith and humbled by divine grace.

Recognizing the multifaceted nature of social justice challenges, Christian conservatives aim to integrate scriptural wisdom with practical action. **As we navigate these complex terrains, we must appreciate that diverse approaches to social justice can coexist. Seeking the common good, after all, is an ambition shared across the spectrum of beliefs.** Rather than polarizing, the conversation around social justice becomes an opportunity for learning, understanding, and perhaps even discovering new collaborations rooted in shared values of dignity, respect, and love for one's neighbor.

Misconceptions Dispelled

Through the diligent examination of Christian conservatism's intersection with social justice, it becomes abundantly clear that the misconception of indifference is unfounded. **Christian conservatives are deeply invested in the pursuit of social justice, albeit through a lens that is intimately tied to Biblical teachings.** One must maintain that justice, along with righteousness, is not only a social mandate but a fundamental aspect of faith.

Let us march forth with the assurance that our path is just, our convictions strong, and our actions aligned with a greater good. Our endeavors, framed by faith and informed by a broad spectrum of knowledge, hold the promise to not only transform hearts but also shape the society in which we live. In this shared journey toward what some call social justice, but we would move towards biblical justice, let the truths we have uncovered in this exploration illuminate your way.

A COMPASSIONATE CRUSADE: COMMUNITY WELL-BEING THROUGH CONSERVATIVE LENSES

Johnathan lingered by the entrance of the sparsely filled community center, a building showing its years in the layered paint peeling off the walls, holding in its frames the laughter and solemn vows of his neighbors. It stood as a sentinel in the small, Southern town where people knew each other not just by name but by history, a place where echoes of spiritual hymns often spilled out of open windows, seeping into the very soil that cradled the roots of grand oak trees.

This afternoon the center hosted a meeting, one of many spurred by ideals usually confined within Sunday sermons, now gaining voice through community action. Johnathan had never been one for the limelight, yet here he was, smoothing out the creases on his blazer, a testament to the pressing weight of necessity over comfort. As he greeted his neighbors, there was a semblance of warmth, yet beneath it, an undercurrent of urgency clung to his firm handshakes. These were hands that had known the rough give of tilled soil and the unyielding resilience of wood, hands that now sought to mold a future wrought by the same determination.

In his heart, there was a fierce allegiance to the teachings that had fortified him from youth – the parables and proverbs that had become not just Scripture but blueprints to a life that valued community and stewardship. Personal responsibility was more than just a creed; it was the constant companion to his daily toil and the anchor through many storms. The room began to fill, the hum of conversation growing like the awakening of a hive, each voice a harbinger of the task they had before them.

Bea, an elder in both the local church and community, pulled him aside. "Johnathan, what you're proposing... It's been tried before. And the wind didn't carry our words far enough." Her gaze was steady, unwavering, a reflection of the wisdom etched by years of watching over her kin.

He offered her a smile, not of naivety, but of resolve. "Aunt Bea, I know. But perhaps it's not the distance of the wind but the readiness of the soil. I believe we're ready to cultivate something lasting, with hands and hearts and something more than just words."

His eyes scanned the room, settling on the young faces, the budding dreams, the untapped potential. The youth, especially, radiated a promise that he yearned to nurture. They would be the ones to carry the baton, to keep it steady, to cross finish lines unimaginable to the prior generations of their parents, grandparents, and great-grandparents.

The community-driven solutions he envisioned were seeds he believed could burgeon into gardens of prosperity, not through the sweeping gestures of governance, but through the painstaking love of those who tilled close to the earth. It was economic development born not from legislation but from the neighborhood workshops and the small businesses near the city center, from the integrity of work and the pride of craftsmanship. It was a pathway paved by the belief that every man and woman was their brother's and sister's keeper.

Each narrative he wove into his speech was a thread connecting the spiritual to the pragmatic, the divine to the achievable. There were nods from the crowd, an affirmation of shared conviction, and in their eyes, a glimmer that mirrored the flickering flame of a candle vigil – soft but steadfast.

As the meeting drew to a close, and conversations began to weave into the fabric of determination, Johnathan stood silently, watching the night cloak the world outside the windows, the stars peering curiously at this pocket of the earth.

What if the seeds sown today, watered by faith and toil, could truly bloom into legacies tomorrow? What does it take for a tree to know its strength lies not in the reach of its branches, but in the unseen depth of its far-reaching roots?

Unearthing the Pillars of Progress

The narrative of Black Christian conservatives is rich with tenets of faith, community, and personal responsibility. At the heart of their beliefs lies an unwavering commitment to furthering the welfare of their society. These individuals understand that fostering community progress is not a monolithic pursuit; it carries the nuances of their lived experiences, cultural history, and spiritual convictions. Unlike solutions steeped in government dependence, Black Christian conservatives advocate for community empowerment that sprouts from within, leveraging personal responsibility and community-driven initiatives as its bedrock.

This stand is predicated on a distinct worldview that sees human dignity and agency as integral to societal advancement. Christian conservative values are not mere philosophical positions but practical imperatives that guide action towards sustainable improvement. These values, deeply rooted in spiritual teachings, endorse the idea that every individual has a role to play in their community's upliftment. They encourage the understanding that each person must cultivate their talents and serve others, thereby creating a ripple effect of improvement that resonates throughout the community.

Adopting strategies that focus on character development, financial stewardship, and social cohesion, this demographic is poised to lay a foundation of self-sufficiency. These strategies emphasize the importance of nurturing a robust work ethic, fostering strong family support systems, and maintaining spiritual fortitude in the face of adversity. In asserting these values, Black Christian conservatives are not only seeking to offer an alternative to excessive government intervention but are also upholding the principles of their faith.

It is essential to analyze and grasp the impact of non-governmental approaches. Numerous instances showcase the efficacy of initiatives led by churches, faith-based organizations, and local leaders in responding to societal needs. By catalyzing community support, these entities have often succeeded where government programs have stalled, tailoring interventions to the unique contexts they serve. The lessons from such forays into community enhancement should not be overlooked but rather investigated for their potential to inform broader policies with best practices to include and replicate.

Central to this discourse is the power of the entrepreneurial spirit, which is celebrated as a driver of economic and social change. By encouraging entrepreneurship within the community, Black Christian conservatives believe that they are not only stimulating economic growth but also fostering a sense of ownership and pride among community members. This, in turn, fuels a more proactive stance towards tackling issues such as chronic unemployment, lack of financial literacy education and low math / reading test scores from our children — issues imperative to the overall health of the community.

In navigating the intersection of spirituality and politics, there's a compelling narrative of resilience and innovation that emerges. The journey of Black Christian conservatives is one of perseverance against the odds, rooted in a faith that acts as a steadfast anchor. Theirs is a living testament to the impact of a community that, despite facing historical and systemic challenges, refuses to blame everything on racism and yet continues to strive for a brighter future crafted by their hands and guided by their faith in God and in each other. The strategies laid out by this vibrant constituency prove that solutions to pressing societal issues can be as diverse as the communities they aim to serve.

The pursuit of community well-being has been a long-standing objective across all political and religious spectrums; however, the manner in which Christian conservatives endeavor towards this goal is often profoundly misunderstood. A cornerstone of the philosophy that guides them is the principle of stewardship — a deep-seated belief in caring for the resources and people within one's community as an act of faith and obligation. **If you are faithful over a few, you can become ruler over many.** This stems from the Biblical teaching that every individual is responsible for what they have been given by God, including the people under their care. Christian conservatives apply this sense of stewardship by investing in institutions and initiatives that empower others with the necessary education, skills and resources to succeed, rather than solely relying on external authorities and hand-outs to enact change.

Community progress under the conservative lens is synonymous with enhancing local support structures. Churches and faith-based organizations frequently become beacons of community assistance, providing not just spiritual guidance but practical support like food banks, job training, and family counseling. This localized, hands-on approach ensures that aid is not only available but also tailored to the specific needs and challenges of the community. The strength of this model lies in its foundation of interpersonal relationships and direct accountability — a personal touch often lost in larger bureaucratic systems.

Moving towards a community-first philosophy, Christian conservatives stress the importance of maintaining the family unit as the primary source of social stability and child development. By nurturing strong family bonds, communities inherently grow stronger. A focus on traditional values serves to reinforce the importance of education, hard work, and moral righteousness, which in turn foster an environment where individuals can flourish and contribute positively to their community. This is not to claim that such values are exclusive to conservative communities, but rather to highlight the different pathways through which they seek to cultivate them.

A thriving community also requires economic vitality, a fundamental tenet for Christian conservatives who promote entrepreneurship and small business growth. The belief here is that by creating opportunities for self-reliance and economic contribution, individuals are able to take on greater personal responsibility and contribute more to the well being and prosperity of their families and communities. Such an investment is not merely financial; it is a moral and ethical

responsibility that showcases faith in action — lifting up one's neighbors through economic empowerment.

Encouraging volunteerism and philanthropy is also integral to fostering well-rounded citizens. When individuals volunteer their time,
talent or treasure, they are not only helping those in need but are
also engaged in a transformational experience that often encourages a
lifetime of service in reciprocity. Community initiatives that arise from
such a spirit of giving can range from mentoring programs and literacy
projects to environmental conservation efforts — each driven by the
intrinsic values of conservative faith that regards service as a means of
grace and community strengthening.

Education also plays a crucial role in the conservative vision for
community progress. Scholarships and educational programs funded
by churches and private donors exemplify the commitment to equip
the next generation with the tools needed for success. By prioritizing education within the community, Christian conservatives aim to
break cycles of poverty and dependency, fostering independence and
equipping individuals with the means to uplift themselves and their
neighbors.

When one contemplates the fabric of a well-tended community
as envisioned by Christian conservatives, it is clear that the emphasis
lies on proactive, hands-on involvement — where the improvement
of lives is achieved through collective effort and personal engagement,
rather than passive expectation. By prioritizing these approaches, they
believe that the most sustainable and meaningful progress is made.

Personal Responsibility: A Cornerstone of Conservative Thought

Within the framework of conservative methodology, personal responsibility emerges as a crucial tenet. This principle is deeply rooted in spiritual teachings that emphasize stewardship over one's life and circumstances. The call to cultivate self-reliance and a sense of ownership not only aligns with biblical wisdom but also empowers the individual to contribute positively to societal well-being. It fosters a sense of ownership — each person investing in the fabric of their community by maintaining integrity in their personal, professional, and civic lives. When individuals embrace personal responsibility, they contribute more meaningfully to their community's infrastructure, from local businesses to social services. These contributions, grounded in a strong moral and ethical framework, drive progress in ways that can often be more adaptable and immediate than those facilitated by the government.

Harnessing Community-Driven Solutions

Engaging the power of the collective is another strategic component in conservative circles. Where some look towards expansive government programs to solve community challenges, conservatives often advocate for grassroots movements as the driving force for meaningful change. This echoes the theme found in the book of Acts, where believers shared among themselves, ensuring none was in need (Acts 4:34). **The underlying belief is that those closest to the issues at hand possess the most pertinent insights and motivation to implement effective solutions.** By encouraging communities to

rally around shared values and challenges, a more tailored and cultur-
ally sensitive approach to problem-solving is achievable — one that
respects autonomy and celebrates local leadership.

The Enterprising Spirit of Conservatism

One cannot discuss conservative methodology without highlighting
the entrepreneurial spirit that underlies it. Convictions about work
and its role in personal development are not merely economic positions but also spiritual affirmations about the innate value and potential within every individual. **As the Bible says in Proverbs 14:23,**
"In all toil there is profit, but mere talk tends only to poverty."
The conservative movement seeks to awaken the entrepreneurial drive
within the community, cultivating businesses and organizations that
reflect core values and serve the greater good. It is a call to action for
individuals to manifest their God-given talents through commerce
and industry, thereby contributing to prosperity and communal upliftment.

Advantages of Non-Governmental Interventions

In a world that often looks first to governmental solutions, conservative strategies present a compelling case for non-governmental approaches. These initiatives, ranging from faith-based charities to community outreach programs, resonate with the teachings of Christ who
emphasized the good Samaritan's personal compassion over institu-
tional responses (Luke 10:25-37). **By engaging in voluntary service**
and philanthropy, communities can address social needs with a
sense of immediacy and personal touch that larger systems may
lack. Additionally, utilizing non-governmental avenues can encourage

innovation, efficiency, and personal involvement — attributes that instill a sense of purpose and fulfillment in those who serve and those who are served.

The Role of Education and Empowerment

Education lies at the heart of empowering individuals to take responsibility for their lives and communities. It's through this empowerment that people can identify their purpose and place within society, channeling their unique gifts in ways that benefit all. By advocating for education that is both enriching and practical, conservative leaders seek to equip individuals with the skills necessary to navigate life's complexities with wisdom and discernment. Whether through charter schools, vocational training, or mentorship programs, the aim is to foster lifelong learners who are well-prepared to make meaningful contributions to community development.

Conclusion

The approach outlined here represents a distinctively conservative path to community well-being, one that cherishes the interplay between personal initiative and communal support. It's a path that trusts in the capacity of individuals and local institutions to identify and address their own needs. Churches and faith-based organizations, in partnership with private enterprises and other non-profit organizations, for example, have long played pivotal roles in creating safety nets for the disadvantaged, launching educational programs, and fostering environments where healing and growth can thrive.

As readers absorb these principles and reflect on their applicability to their own contexts, it's hoped that they will see the transformative potential of these strategies and be inspired to implement them in their quests for societal betterment. The journey toward a community that flourishes on every level is not swift or simple, but with faith as the anchor, it is an endeavor that resonates with promise and profound purpose.

A TAPESTRY OF BELIEFS: THE SPECTRUM OF BLACK CHRISTIAN CONSERVATISM

In the warmth of a Wednesday afternoon, Naomi sat in the corner booth of a small cafe, one frequented by those who valued solitude and a good cup of coffee. Her laptop lay open before her, the cursor blinking steadily on a blank document. Thoughts that echoed the diverse vocalizations of conservative Christianity murmured in her mind, forming a silent choir harmonizing with the soft jazz in the background. All the while, the scent of roasted beans provided a comforting embrace as she pondered the delicate balance of unity and diversity.

She sipped her coffee, its bitterness mingling with the sweet caramel notes, much like the blend of conservative values and progressive social justice efforts that stirred within her. Naomi, a seasoned entrepreneur, chewed gently on the end of her pen, contemplating the construction of her next workshop aimed at nurturing leadership in her community. Guided by her faith and the subtle wisdom of her grandmother's teachings, she aspired to bridge the gaps that too often separated like minds on the basis of interpretative differences.

A gentleman to her left laughed heartily, his round spectacles catching the light as he shared a story with his companion, a young man who hung on every word. Naomi noted the ease with which their conversation flowed, the older imparting knowledge with confidence, the younger receiving it with a blend of respect and curiosity. It was a testament to the cross-generational discourse she hoped to foster. She jotted down a note, linking theology, politics, and economics — each a thread in the intricate tapestry of community engagement.

Naomi reflected on a forum from the previous week, where she witnessed a fiery debate diffuse into a warm understanding, much like the heat of her coffee dissipating into the coolness of the cafe's air. She held fast to the belief that it was not uniformity but the richness of varied experiences that would propel her people forward. How, she wondered, could she harness the fervor of these voices, shaping them into a melody of action while preserving their individual tones?

With the sun lowering outside, casting orange hues on the crisp tablecloth, Naomi mulled over the distinction between the philosophical underpinnings of Biblical interpretation and the tangible actions they prompted. She knew all too well that for her and her fellow parishioners, their faith deeply rooted in the wisdom of the scriptures, was not merely for reflection but a call to action, visible in the way they conducted their businesses, raised their children, and participated in the political realm.

As the sky shifted its palette, dusk cloaking the city in a gentle hush, a spark of clarity alighted upon her thoughts. She typed, her fingers moving with new conviction, describing a vision where different voices could resonate in a single chorus, advocating for respect and strides in commerce without losing the essence of individual belief.

Naomi closed her laptop, her document now filled with a plan both unifying and electrifying. Will this blueprint of hers, infused with the convictions of generations and the anticipation of change, resonate with the hearts of leaders eager to craft a future that honors the past while boldly stepping into the new?

Unveiling the Spectrum: The Rich Diversity of Black Christian Conservatism

The landscape of Black Christian conservatism is anything but monochromatic. Often perceived through a simplistic lens, its spiritual contours and political nuances reveal a complex tapestry of vibrant beliefs and practices. Diverse in interpretation and varied in action, this demographic exemplifies a conservative tradition that is both deeply rooted in scripture and dynamically engaged in modern society. It is through this prism of faith and action that a movement emerges, one that beckons its followers to uphold sacred truths while actively shaping the socio-political fabrics of their communities.

Readers will discover, in these pages, an eye-opening exposition of the manifold ways in which Black Christian conservatives deal with the Biblical texts and cultural contexts. The scope ranges from unwavering literalism to more dynamic, interpretative approaches. This diversity echoes a broader, more profound conversation on how immutable truths apply in the shifting sands of contemporary life. This variance is not an indicator of discord, but rather a display of the rich intellectual and spiritual life within the community.

Moreover, this chapter unveils the multitudes within Black Christian conservatism that stand along a spectrum of political engagement. Some choose the path of deliberate separation, while others leap into the political arena with verve and vigilance. Recognizing the complexity of these political stances is key to understanding the broader movement's influence on policy and public life. Such awareness facilitates not just an academic grasp but opens a doorway to genuine engagement and dialogue within and beyond conservative circles.

The cornerstone of unity amidst diversity is emphasized here, not as a mere aspiration but as a foundational principle that safeguards the community's integrity. Readers will learn that, despite a plurality of voices, there is a shared commitment to unity that transcends individual differences. This solidarity is celebrated not in spite of the spectrum of beliefs and actions, but precisely because of it. By understanding this, participants in the Black Christian conservative movement can navigate disagreements with grace and extend the table of brotherhood wider than ever before.

As you embark on a journey through the rich landscape of Black Christian conservatism, you will encounter a compelling and diverse array of interpretations and practices that span a wide spectrum. At one end, there are those who adhere to a **strict literalism**, interpreting the Bible with an unwavering eye and regarding every verse as an unchallengeable edict. They are the sentinels of tradition, whose firm grasp of scriptural tenets forms the bedrock of their beliefs and lifestyle choices.

Moving along the spectrum, another group takes a more **contextual approach**, weaving historical and cultural understanding into their readings of the sacred texts. For them, the Bible is not just a collection of rules but a living document that resonates with the evolving experiences and challenges of the Black community. They find in its passages a means to address the contemporary struggles they face, from social injustice to personal triumphs, believing that spirituality should be as dynamic as the lives they lead.

Amidst these interpretations, a third faction has emerged. These are the **progressive conservatives**, who seek to harmonize their deep-seated Christian values with a rapidly changing world. They understand that faith must sometimes adapt to remain relevant, blending long standing doctrines with new insights to better serve their communities and the greater good. While their flexibility can attract criticism from purists, their adaptability is a testament to the resilience and creativity inherent to this multifaceted group.

Among the three categories, I would classify myself closer to a strict literalist that believes that what the Bible says is true and infallible. As a strong advocate for biblical literacy, I affirm that the Bible is the Word of God and is the objective standard of truth, based on what God says is right and wrong. I also seek to understand the context at the time and setting of the writings of each book, so I have a better understanding of what God and the human authors meant to write to the audiences at the time. From there, I would exegete what the text is saying and seek to apply what the author originally said to the current time and situation that I and my audience - if I am preaching - are experiencing now.

But interpretations are only one facet of this intricate tapestry. Practices among Black Christian conservatives reveal just as much variety. Some observe a rigorous regimen of church attendance, Bible study, and prayer, finding solace in the regular rhythms of worship. To them, these are not mere rituals but vital sources of strength and renewal, avenues to maintain a close connection with their faith.

In contrast, others integrate their spirituality more seamlessly into everyday life, seeing the reflection of their beliefs in the way they conduct their business, nurture their families, and engage with their communities. For them, faith is in action, animated not by the number of services they attend, but by the daily deeds that mirror the teachings of Christ. This lived expression of Christianity showcases the practical application of faith principles as a foundation for personal conduct and ethical decision-making.

Despite the differences, a common thread unites these various strands: a shared belief in the transformative power of faith. Whether through strict adherence to doctrine or innovative interpretations and practices, these believers are united by their devotion to a Christianity that shapes and informs their identity. Through their faith, they seek to contribute meaningfully to the world, championing a narrative of hope, perseverance, and moral clarity.

As we unpack the diverse engagements and responses to political and social issues in the next segment, it becomes clear that this faith, with all its textures and shades, is not a monolith. It is a vibrant, living expression of eclectic beliefs and actions that reflect the richness of the Black Christian conservative community.

Bridging Faith and Civic Duty: The Varied Political Perspectives of Black Christian Conservatives

Within the realm of Black Christian conservatism, political engagement is as varied as the hues of a sunset. Each individual brings their unique convictions to bear on their civic responsibilities, demonstrating a rich tapestry of ideologies and actions. **It is not uncommon to find some Black Christian conservatives who wholly eschew political involvement, seeking instead to create change through spiritual revival and community outreach**. They believe that the most effective transformation begins in the heart and that policy shifts are secondary to moral and spiritual renewal.

Conversely, there is a significant cohort among Black Christian conservatives actively lobbying for political reform and

legislative action. These individuals view the political arena as a critical battleground for the values they hold dear, such as sanctity of life, traditional family structures, and educational choice. They invest time, resources, and effort into campaigns, voting, and even seeking public office, reflecting their conviction that faith and governance can, indeed, work hand in hand.

Amidst these two poles, myriad perspectives exist. Some prioritize economic policies in line with conservative ideas, centering on entrepreneurship, economic empowerment, and fiscal responsibility as tools for improving the lives of individuals and communities alike. They weave together their understanding of scriptural teachings on stewardship with practical economic principles to advocate for what they consider to be Biblically-infused economic wisdom.

Another thread within the spectrum includes those focused on social issues such as prison reform, education, and healthcare, often highlighting systemic injustices that disproportionately affect the Black community. Although they may align with conservative philosophies, they vigorously pursue social justice, ensuring that their efforts reflect a holistic understanding of the scripture's call to *"act justly and to love mercy and to walk humbly with your God"* (Micah 6:8).

There are also those within this community who take a pragmatic approach to politics, often aligning with policies or parties that they feel best represent Biblical principles, regardless of the traditional conservative or liberal labels. They underscore the importance of wisdom and discernment in evaluating each issue on its own merits and seek to engage thoughtfully with a range of political ideas.

It's important to note that within this pluralistic landscape, Black Christian conservatives often face unique social pressures and challenges. Their political choices and engagement strategies may set them apart from broader trends within their religious or racial communities, leading them to navigate complex societal dynamics that require fortitude and resilience, traits that are cultivated through both spiritual practice and communal support.

The common thread that binds this diverse group is the pursuit of a society that reflects their fundamental beliefs — beliefs that are steeped in a reverence for the Bible, a commitment to personal faith, and a desire to see Christian principles inform all areas of life, including politics. Despite the differences in how this mission is implemented, the shared vision is for a society where moral integrity and divine wisdom are reflected in the halls of power and the common good.

In fostering this vision, Black Christian conservatives look to leverage their influence in ways that shepherd their communities towards greater stability, morality, and prosperity. This involves not only advocating for policies and leaders that resonate with their values but also serving as examples of those values through personal integrity, community service, and responsible citizenship.

Overall, this multifaceted presence in the political sphere serves as a reminder that Black Christian conservatism is not a monolith, but rather a dynamic force with the potential to make substantial contributions to the public discourse and the shaping of societal norms. Their varied inclinations underline the importance of understanding and respecting the different ways in which faith informs political engagement.

Amidst the conversations and the healthy debates among Christians within the Black community, let it be known that our differences are not a hurdle but a strength. They inspire us to engage with rigor, to listen with empathy, and to embrace each other's perspectives with the love modeled by Christ. In the business of living out our faith, these variances become opportunities — to innovate, to challenge, to grow, and to pursue excellence in all that we do, for the glory of God.

Let such a community stand not in contradiction but in jubilant affirmation of Psalm 133:1 – *"Behold, how good and how pleasant it is for brethren to dwell together in unity!"* It is in our harmonic diversities that we find the resonance of true community, enduring through all seasons and reflecting the manifold wisdom of God to the world. As mentors, leaders, and followers, our shared journey is one of continuous learning, critical reflection, and spirited engagement. We advance not only our individual ambitions but also the collective well-being of our broader community, embodying the entrepreneurial spirit that takes faith beyond the church walls and into the vibrant tapestry of our lives.

GUIDING THE PATH: SKILLFUL NAVIGATION OF CONSERVATIVE CHRISTIAN BELIEFS

J ohnathan stood on the front porch, the brisk morning air mingling with the dew-laden breath of earth and the warmth of a rising sun painting a serene horizon. He grasped the day's mail — a mix of local newspapers and political flyers, all seemingly pleading for attention. With a silent prayer, he sought wisdom beyond the ink and paper, wisdom rooted in the ancient text that lay open on his kitchen table each morning.

Yesterday's town hall debate lingered in his mind, a mosaic of opinions, a clash between progress and tradition. He remembered hands clasped firmly as the crowd whispered among themselves, searching for an anchor in the words of their representatives. Johnathan recalled the firmness in his own voice as he had spoken, resolute yet kind, drawing on Scripture as much as on civic knowledge to articulate his stance.

The sun rose higher, pouring gold over his modest garden, reminding him of the parables of growth and nurturing. He recognized the parallels — his community, like the delicate flowers and sturdy vegetables, required care, informed by both faith and reason. Stepping back into his home, he brushed his fingertips across the spines of well-worn books, a collection bridging Augustine and Adam Smith, each page a testament to the balanced view he strove to maintain.

Inside, the scent of polished wood mingled with a hint of dried lavender from the small sachets his wife placed about the house. A stack of community newsletters lay on the counter next to an array of highlighted verses — a roadmap not just for his soul, but for engaging with others. He pondered the upcoming gathering at the church, where neighborhood plans would intertwine with Bible readings, seeking resonance in the hearts of those who shared his values.

The clock ticked gently in the silent living room, a metronomic reminder that there were hours to fill before tonight's panel discussion. Jonathan would stand before an eager audience, sharing insights on resilient faith in a secular world. As he turned his gaze back to the blue sky framed by the open window, his thoughts wandered to the youth, how they navigated the tides of cultural change, how they balanced the compass of faith with the map of modernity. Would they find the same solace in ancient wisdom, he wondered, or would they carve out new paths to understanding?

The Compass for a Conservative Christian

In the ever-swirling currents of modern socio-political discourse, navigating the waters of conservative Christian beliefs demands not just conviction, but the mastery of specific navigational tools. Scripture, often the bedrock of Christian conservatism, requires a robust literacy to understand and articulate its nuances. **Biblical literacy** is more than familiarity — it is the ability to dissect, comprehend, and connect ancient teachings with contemporary dilemmas, forging an unshakeable foundation for one's beliefs.

Yet this journey is not meant to be walked alone. The church and its associated communities are vessels designed for mutual edification and support. Thus, **community engagement** emerges as a critical skill, allowing one to build strong collaborative relationships while upholding foundational values. It is within these alliances that conservative Christians find support and the collective strength to voice their convictions.

Effective communication is the rudder guiding these efforts, skillfully steering conversations in a manner that resonates with both conservative principles and the broader spectrum of beliefs. This requires an empathetic ear and a disciplined tongue, ensuring that dialogues foster understanding without compromising on core values. Coupled with political awareness, Christians can engage in informed advocacy, participating in the civic arena with insight and impact.

Inner resilience, born from a deep wellspring of faith, allows believers to withstand external pressures without buckling. This spiritual fortitude emboldens the conservative Christian to stand firm, even amidst the tides of popular opinion or political change. Meanwhile, **reconciliation skills** act as the lifeline for bridging divides, seeking harmony without surrendering the essence of one's convictions and worldview.

When these skills are honed, the conservative Christian is well-equipped to maintain their convictions in a society that often challenges them. It is a dance of grace and grit, requiring the individual to remain rooted in their faith while navigating through the complex dynamics of a more secular and, at times, more hostile world towards Christianity.

The Tapestry of Conversation and Belonging

The challenge of preserving robust conservative values within diverse communities extends beyond personal fortitude; it requires tactful interaction and a gentleness of spirit that invites rather than alienates. Scriptural commandments to love one's neighbor as oneself become intertwined with the call to speak the truth in love. This delicate balance mandates a skillful approach to conversation — an approach that begins with active listening and culminates in conveying one's message with clarity and respect.

Engagement within the community serves a dual purpose. On one hand, it affirms the individual's commitment to conservative Christian principles through participation in collective actions. On the other, it opens the door to serve others, thereby building bridges of understanding and mutual respect. Through such engagement, one's life becomes a testimony, embodying the values espoused by their faith.

On the political front, the acquisition of **awareness and discernment** facilitates engagement with policy and law in a manner that aligns with moral convictions. It empowers believers to contribute to discussions on governance and societal structures, ensuring that their perspectives are informed, poignant, and contextually relevant. This awareness goes hand-in-hand with resilience, enabling Christians to navigate political climates that fluctuate with the ebb and flow of cultural trends.

Inner resilience stands as the bulwark against the assault of discouragement, criticism or weariness. A well-nurtured spiritual life not only nourishes personal growth but also reinforces the capacity to engage with compassion and conviction. It is this internal well of strength and hope that enables the conservative Christian to face opposition without losing heart, looking to Jesus as the perfect example.

The Bridge of Reconciliation

As conservative Christians stand firm in their beliefs, they are often met with the challenge of reconciling their worldview with an increasingly pluralistic society. Here, it becomes essential to foster strategies for reconciliation that do not compromise core values. The artful practice of reconciliation acknowledges differences while simultaneously seeking common ground — a place where dialogue can continue and relationships can flourish.

The chapter ahead is more than a set of rules; it is an invitation to exercise wisdom and courage in daily interactions. It aims to equip readers with the tools to sensitively and effectively uphold their conservative principles, fostering spaces where faith can thrive, unabated by the complexities of a diverse and often contentious world.

This careful negotiation between faith and interaction challenges conservative Christians to refine their approach to testimony and influence. The skills and strategies mentioned are not just assets — they are essential armaments for those seeking to live out their faith authentically and influentially in the modern era. Thus equipped, believers can navigate their journey with confidence, knowing that they possess the requisite knowledge, skills, and heart to weather the voyage.

In the quest to uphold conservative Christian beliefs, it is imperative that believers are well-versed in the very foundation of those beliefs

— the **Bible. Biblical literacy is not merely the ability to recite verses from memory, but to comprehend the tenets, context, and history of the Biblical narrative.** This enriches one's faith and provides a robust framework against which contemporary issues can be assessed. As such, engaging regularly in both personal and group Bible study becomes a vital activity, ensuring that beliefs are not just inherited but owned and understood.

Political awareness, while seemingly secular, complements Biblical literacy in the life of a conservative Christian. **One must grasp the complexity of the political landscape and recognize where faith intersects with policy. This knowledge empowers believers to make informed decisions at the ballot box, and more importantly, to advocate for legislation that mirrors Biblical principles.** This awareness extends to local, state, and federal levels because as stewards of society, Christians are called to actively participate not only through prayer but also through practical civic engagement.

Effective navigation of these realms requires an ability to discern truth from misinformation. In an era where both media and personal biases can obscure facts, it's critical for conservative Christians to engage with a range of credible sources. Developing critical thinking skills enables one to analyze and understand various viewpoints without compromising core beliefs. This intellectual rigor protects one from being swayed by eloquent rhetoric that lacks substance or truth.

Apart from gathering knowledge, application of that knowledge is where the true test of conviction lies. It's essential to put scriptural and political insights into practice by integrating them into daily interactions and decision-making processes. It's not enough to know what the Bible says or to understand the political climate; one must live out those convictions through acts of kindness, justice, and integrity — becoming a living testimony of the belief system one upholds.

However, acquiring these skills should never be done in isolation. **Community** plays an integral role in refining and sharpening one's beliefs and practices. Surrounding oneself with a supportive network offers both accountability and encouragement. Joining or forming groups that hold similar values can provide a space for discussion, accountability, debate, and growth, which is beneficial for deepening one's understanding and resilience.

One must also be prepared to engage with those who challenge or question conservative Christian viewpoints. **This engagement should be marked by grace, respect, and openness to dialogue. While staying firm in one's beliefs, it is equally important to listen and respond thoughtfully rather than react defensively**. This builds bridges and communicates the love and wisdom at the heart of Christian doctrine.

Lastly, one needs to constantly align one's life with the Scriptures and seek wisdom through prayer. The guidance of the Holy Spirit cannot be overstated in navigating the complexities of aligning conservative Christian beliefs in a diverse society that is regularly engaged in spiritual warfare. By committing to a life of learning, engagement, and spiritual discipline, believers can be both gracious and steadfast ambassadors of Jesus Christ.

Fostering Communication: Bridging Belief with Dialogue

Effective communication is at the heart of navigating conservative Christian beliefs, especially when conversing within a community that holds different views. To communicate effectively, it's essential to strike a balance between articulating your values and showing respect for others' opinions. One practical tip is to listen first, allowing others to express their thoughts before sharing your own. This not only fosters a sense of respect but also offers the opportunity to understand where they're coming from, which can inform a more empathetic and effective response.

Cultivate Empathy in Your Dialogue

When engaging with community members, empathy is key. **Rather than approaching discussions with the aim of convincing others, enter conversations with the intent to understand and connect.** This does not mean compromising on beliefs but recognizing the humanity in those you interact with. Sharing personal anecdotes that illustrate your values can bridge gaps and humanize your perspectives. For instance, recall moments when your faith provided strength in the face of adversity or when conservative principles proved beneficial in your own life.

Build Bridges Through Community Involvement

An undeniable way to demonstrate the positive impact of conservative Christian values is through active participation in community projects. **Volunteering not only exemplifies Christ's teachings on service but also places you within the context of civic engagement, where actions often speak louder than words.** Whether it's supporting local charities, mentoring young people or getting involved in school programs, your involvement showcases the practical application of your faith and beliefs.

Navigating the political landscape requires a deft understanding of how faith intersects with public policies. **Stay informed about local, state, and national issues, and consider how Biblical principles**

inform your viewpoints on these matters. Engage in political discussions by highlighting how conservative values can address social concerns, emphasizing not just the morality but also the logic and effectiveness of these approaches.

Fostering Resilience in Faith and Conviction

Resilience is essential when your views are in the minority, and it begins with a solid foundation in your beliefs. Ground yourself in spiritual disciplines like prayer, solitude and regular Bible study, which not only fortify your convictions but also provide peace amidst discord. It's essential to cultivate an inner strength that sustains your resolve to live out your faith authentically with Jesus Christ as your anchor.

In conversations that could escalate to debates, maintaining a calm demeanor and speaking with clarity and kindness can diffuse tension and leave a lasting, positive impression. While you should be firm in your convictions, your tone should be gentle, reflecting the grace that is a cornerstone of the Christian faith. As the Bible says in Colossians 4:5-6: *"Walk in wisdom toward outsiders, making the best use of the time. Let your speech always be gracious, seasoned with salt, so that you may know how you ought to answer each person."*

Harness the Power of Reconciliation

Reconciliation is a powerful skill when navigating conservative Christian beliefs within a broader community. Aim for constructive dialogues that promote understanding and healing, rather than division. **Reconciliatory communication does not shy away from discussing core beliefs; rather, it seeks common ground and focuses**

on shared values, such as the importance of family, the need for ethical governance, or the pursuit of justice.

Finally, remember that becoming adept at articulating and defending your conservative Christian worldview is a continuous process. As you share in loving fellowship with others, be gracious towards one another, stay humble, be willing to learn, and let your life be a testament to your faith. Actions often resonate louder than words, and a life lived in alignment with your beliefs can have a profound impact on those around you, sometimes more than the most eloquent argument.

Concluding Thoughts

Remember, the endeavor before us is multifaceted, but by embracing the strategies discussed, you are well-equipped to make a difference. Allow your understanding of scriptures to be the compass by which you navigate, and let your awareness of the political landscape empower you to act judiciously. Engage with your community in a manner that reflects the love and strength of your convictions, and be an example of resilience in the face of opposition. Carry forward the intent to reconcile differences, and in doing so, your life will be a testament to the transformative power of living your faith boldly and without compromise.

Armed with these insights and the spirit of God as your guide, step confidently into the world. Encourage one another, be steadfast in your beliefs, and contribute to the tapestry of our societal values with grace and intelligence. As you close this chapter, let the lessons herein fuel your voyage ahead, imbuing each step with purpose and conviction. Your journey of navigating conservatism as a Christian within the Black community is a powerful narrative of faith in action, painting a picture to the world of what is possible when we hold fast to what we believe, identifying first with Jesus over our blackness.

Embrace this path with both courage and humility, knowing that you are part of a larger story — one that is enriched by your unique voice and unwavering commitment.

STEELED IN SPIRIT: FOSTERING RESILIENCE AMONGST RESISTANCE

In the heart of an unassuming enclave, where the rhythmic pulses of life unfolded beneath the deep vermilion of a setting sun, Mariah stood firm outside the ramshackle walls of what the locals called the "Meeting House." The air around her carried the savory hint of a distant barbecue mingled with the soft, earthy scent of pine. Horses nickered from a nearby field, their hooves stomping with impatience as if echoing Mariah's own restless spirit. In this moment, she was an island within her community, isolated not by oceans but by beliefs.

Mariah's hands, rough from years of relentless labor, held a worn Bible against her chest — a shield in a battle of conviction. As voices swelled from within the Meeting House, a cacophony of passionate discourse, she recalled her grandmother's words, spoken with the cadence of enduring wisdom, "Faith is the spine of life, child. Stand tall, even when the storm rages." She pondered the clash of ideals at the last supper she attended, where men and women, some she called kin, challenged her conservative Christian values. They branded them as relics, out of step with the broader perspectives that now permeated even the quiet corners of this southern town.

The notion of opposition within her community clung to her thoughts, stubborn as the red clay clinging to the hem of her dress. It wasn't merely a rejection of ideas but an unspoken question of her very identity. She wrapped her doubts and fears in silent prayer, seeking solace not from the eyes of her neighbors but from the unwavering gaze of the divine.

In her search for reinforcement, Mariah envisioned a network of support akin to the interlaced branches of the oak under which she sought refuge. This envisioned community would be her fortress, bolstering her convictions like the steadfast roots of that ancient tree. As she clung to this hope, she resolved that the path ahead would be forged by resilience — an inner strength that would bloom from the deep well of her faith.

The sunset spilled amber hues across the sky as Mariah stepped towards the Meeting House doors. The golden light haloed her silhouette, painting her as a figure of quiet determination amidst the encroaching shadow. Inside, challenges awaited — opinions to be voiced and dialogues to be had. Mariah entered not just as a participant, but as a testament to a belief unshaken, carrying the torch of her convictions into the gathering night.

Does she not, among the few but resolute, find strength in numbers, or is her resilience the lone, but burgeoning flower in an unforeseen spring?

A Beacon of Conviction Amidst the Tempest

Navigating the pervasive currents of societal expectations can be especially challenging for those whose values are etched within conservative Christian principles. Those in the Black community who align with such ideals often find themselves in a maelstrom of opposition, tasked with the heavy burden of standing unwavering while the gales of popular opinion and secular opposition try to bend their stance. It's a scenario that demands a robust steeled spirit, one that is fortified through deep-rooted belief and the encouragement that comes from fellowship and mutual understanding. At the core of this struggle is a resilient mindset — one that not only understands and identifies the sources of opposition but also thrives in the face of such resistance.

In the pursuit of maintaining conservative Christian beliefs, the Black community may confront several sources of opposition. It's crucial to recognize that these challenges can emanate from both outside of the community — spanning the political and social spectrums — and from within, as varying interpretations of faith and practice come into play. Acknowledging these complexities is the first step to formulating a strategic and spiritual response to them.

Cultivating inner resilience is not merely an abstract ideal; it is a practical strategy that involves reinforcing one's convictions through continuous reflection, prayer, and engagement with the Word. This process nurtures a sense of peace and assurance that cannot be shaken by the ebb and flow of societal peer pressure. Fortifying faith in this way empowers individuals to navigate the complexities of their unique journey with confidence and poise.

Support systems are integral to sustaining individuals who stand by their conservative convictions. These networks provide not only a sense of community but also act as a resource for guidance and encouragement. From congregational settings to online communities, the bonds formed through shared values can serve as a bulwark against the tides of conformity and criticism. Engaging in conversations with like-minded peers offers both comfort and a collective wisdom that can be instrumental in addressing the multifaceted challenges faced.

Faith, fundamentally, is the cornerstone upon which this resilience is constructed. Integrating teachings from respected spiritual texts will illustrate how anchoring oneself in their profound wisdom provides a wellspring of strength. On this foundation, we build the fortitude to remain constant in our convictions, regardless of the relentless winds of societal change. With every step taken on this path, we affirm a legacy of resilience that both honors the past and paves the way for a future framed by conviction and grace.

United in Spirit, Unwavering in Purpose

Our journey is replete with moments calling for both introspection and action. As we continue to explore the intricate dance between internal fortitude and external resistance, let us be reminded that it is the strength of our spirit that ultimately propels us forward. In the fabric of our collective resolve, each individual thread of conviction contributes to a tapestry of resilience that triumphs over the transient nature of opposition. With faith as our compass and community as our support, we step boldly into the realm of steadfast purpose, embodying the values we cherish most deeply.

Understanding the Sources of Opposition

The journey of a Black conservative Christian is often met with unique challenges within his or her own community. As these individuals navigate their faith and political beliefs, they may encounter opposition from various sources, including historical, cultural, and media-influenced narratives that can, at times, be at odds with conservative values. This opposition is not merely a social inconvenience but can translate into a profound sense of isolation and misunderstanding that goes to the very core of one's identity.

The Black community, rich in history and tradition, has long been associated with a collective movement toward social justice and equality. Inherent within this movement are certain progressive ideologies that are widely assumed to align with the interests of the community. As such, Black Christians who hold conservative views may find themselves in opposition to the predominantly liberal political leanings presumed to be universally accepted by their racial peers. This dynamic places them at the edge of a cultural precipice where their beliefs can often be mischaracterized as contrary to the fight for racial justice and equality.

Mainstream media outlets and entertainment can bolster this divide, shaping public discourse and opinions. They hold considerable power in defining narratives and biases which impact how conservative beliefs are perceived. This is especially pronounced concerning issues of morality, economic policies, and the size and scope of government, where Black conservative voices are frequently underrepresented or misrepresented, crystallizing a monolithic view of Black political consciousness that may not reflect the diversity of thought present within the Black community.

Furthermore, influential figures in the community, such as religious leaders, activists, and political representatives, can serve as barometers for acceptable thought and behavior. **When these figures predominantly espouse liberal perspectives, the suggestion is that to deviate from these views is to deviate from the Black community itself.** Consequently, Black conservative Christians must often defend their perspectives not only to their external critics but also within their places of worship and kinship, where one might expect a sanctuary of shared faith and values.

Engaging with Differing Perspectives

Despite these sources of friction, it is critical for Black conservative Christians to engage thoughtfully with opposing views. Dissonance can serve as an impetus for growth and a deeper understanding of one's convictions. Through respectful discourse and the sharing of perspectives, there is an opportunity to promote consideration and, possibly, change. It is through these meaningful interactions that misconceptions can be addressed, allowing for a more comprehensive view of the pluralistic ideologies that reside within the Black community.

It is important to note that while the opposition to one's beliefs may be based on entrenched narratives or social pressures, it does not inherently make these alternative viewpoints less valid or unworthy of consideration. Rather, the challenge lies in maintaining the fortitude to represent one's own beliefs while allowing space for the beliefs of others to be heard and understood. In walking this tightrope, the Black conservative Christian must find ways to embody resilience, ensuring their own beliefs are given the respect and voice they merit in the broader conversation.

Fostering Respectful Dialogues

To cultivate resilience and retain one's convictions amidst opposition, Black conservative Christians must not only be well-versed in their own beliefs but also in the philosophies of those who disagree with them. An understanding of the historical and social contexts that shape different viewpoints can create avenues for dialogue that are rooted in mutual respect and empathy. Dialogue that demonstrates a comprehension of both sides of an argument is far more compelling and offers a foundation for meaningful progress and mutual understanding.

Embracing Difficult Conversations with Grace

Interacting with differing viewpoints is inevitable, and often, it is through these interactions that resilience gets tested. **Engaging in difficult conversations requires grace and a tempered spirit, hallmarks of Christlike demeanor.** It is not solely about defending one's perspective but doing so with empathy and understanding. Through these exchanges, resilience is honed as it carries forward the hope of respectful dialogue and the possibility of influencing others positively. Christian conservatives can use these moments to demonstrate the strength of their convictions, coupled with the compassion and love inherent in their beliefs.

Intellectual Rigor and Theological Understanding

The dynamics of resilience extend beyond spiritual tenacity; they also encompass an intellectual rigor and deep theological understanding.

Engaging with the Word diligently, studying apologetics, and understanding the socio-political landscapes in which these beliefs operate add layers of sophistication to one's convictions. This intellectual backbone ensures that the resilience is not blind faith but an informed stance, capable of withstanding scrutiny and offering cogent, respectful rebuttals to opposition.

Leading By Example

Leadership plays a pivotal role in cultivating resilience. **Modeling conviction and resilience in leadership — whether in church settings, community organizations, or family life — inspires others to do the same.** It is the conduct of those in leadership that often sets the standard for others within the community. When leaders stand firm in their beliefs with integrity, it paves the way for others to follow suit, understanding that their convictions have merit and are worth upholding. In this way, resilience spreads and becomes an embedded characteristic of the community.

Persistent Prayer as a Foundation

Finally, resilience grows from a steadfast prayer life. **Persistent prayer underscores the reliance on divine intervention and guidance in all matters. It humbles the individual, reminding them of the source of their strength and the importance of continuous communion with God.** Prayer fortifies the spirit against discouragement and bolsters the resolve to face opposition with a balanced heart and mind. Whether in moments of solitude or gathered prayer, it is this connection to God that sustains and invigorates, ensuring that the internal flame of conviction never dims.

Cultivating Conviction and Inner Strength

The journey to cultivate inner resilience begins with self-reflection and a commitment to one's convictions. **When confronted with resistance, it is the knowledge of who we are and whose we are that serves as the ultimate protection.** Real-world experience teaches us that the most authentic form of resilience stems from a place of deep conviction, nurtured by a relationship with Jesus Christ and an understanding of His will for our lives.

Let us not underestimate the value of a supportive community – a network of like-minded individuals who act as pillars of encouragement and sources of wisdom. Engage in dialogue with those who can mentor, offer guidance, and affirm your principles. In the mesh of life's complexities, may we always find solace and reinforcement in the fellowship of the faithful.

Embracing the Path Ahead

The strategies for fostering resilience discussed here are more than theoretical notions; they are tangible practices that have proven effective time and again. We must employ them with vigor and commitment, knowing that it is not only our right but our responsibility to live out our beliefs authentically and wholeheartedly for Jesus Christ.

Remember, the path of the Christian conservative in the Black community is a distinguished one, marked by the courage to stand against the current. It is a journey that demands our full engagement and our unshakable faith — **a journey that we pursue not in isolation, but hand in hand with the Almighty and our supportive brethren in Christ.**

Let each step we take be guided by the wisdom of the Scriptures and reinforced by the fellowship of the faithful. As we impart these insights, may they serve as a source of strength for you, the reader, as you navigate the complex landscape of balancing spiritual and political harmony. Let us move forward with the assured knowledge that our spirit, tempered by trials and steeped in faith, is the very essence of resilience that will lead us to triumph.

HARMONIZING HERITAGE AND HEARTFELT CONVICTIONS

T he morning sun cast a golden hue on the antique storefronts of the small town, where whispers of heritage mingled with the scent of aged wood and history. Amidst the rows of nostalgia, there was one store that stood as a testament to the passage of time, its windows adorned with trinkets that held stories of their own. Inside, James, the proprietor and a man of deep faith, polished a silver cross that had seen scores of Sundays. It wasn't just another artifact; for him, it was a beacon of the ancient and the eternal.

Having inherited this realm of memory from his father, a weight rested on his shoulders — a weight not of oppression but of purpose. The shop, brimming with echoes of bygone eras, was more than a business; it was a microcosm of his identity, his sanctuary where faith and commerce held a silent truce. Each day, he navigated through the delicate dance of honoring his conservative principles while welcoming a world that spun ever faster toward ideals that challenged his own.

James's thoughts often wandered to his childhood spent amidst these very aisles, under the tender guidance of his father who taught him the virtues of diligence and integrity. The teachings from Proverbs 12:24, *"the hand of the diligent shall bear rule,"* rang with clarity in his mind. Now, as he faced the crossroads of preserving tradition in a modern marketplace, those words buffered him against the winds of change.

With each chime of the shop door, came the promise of interaction, of shared stories with customers who sought more than just a purchase — they sought a connection. The cross, back in its rightful place, gleamed brighter as if resonating with his contemplation. There was a harmony to be found, James mused, in sustaining one's essence while engaging in the larger tapestry of the community. His was a ministry through service; his authenticity, the currency he traded as much as the antiques that lined the shelves.

And so, the ambiance of the shop nourished not only James but also those who visited, each leaving with a fraction of the spirit that lingered in the air — a spirit of continuity amidst change. It was a delicate balance, his small act of rebellion against the drumbeat of conformity. As he flicked through the pages of an aged ledger, its lettering as crisp as the day it was inked, he knew his endeavor was as much about preserving his heritage as it was about providing for the present.

In the stillness that followed the departure of his last customer, the golden light now a soft amber, James pondered — was the true measure of success found in the profit columns of his ledger, or in the quiet satisfaction of knowing that, in this corner of the world, he was a guardian of both faith and legacy? How, he wondered, could others find their path to such a junction, where the heart's compass pointed to both the old and the new?

Unraveling the Tension Between Tradition and Truth

At the core of this vital discussion lies the undeniable quest for balance
— how the Black Christian conservative can navigate the tightrope
of cultural expectations and personal convictions. This chapter delves
deep into the heart of such a journey. As members of a rich and diverse
community, balancing the scales between faith-based conservative values and cultural heritage is no mere afterthought; it's a strategic act of
self-preservation and authenticity. **The world often presents a false
dichotomy, suggesting that to be true to one's community, one
must adapt to dominant ideologies. However, the reality is that
holding fast to faith-based conservative principles is not only
possible but offers a path to a more integrated and authentic
existence.**

Faith is not bound by the constraints of popular opinion or fleeting societal trends. It is an anchor, steadfast and enduring. It is also
deeply personal and oftentimes at odds with the prevailing winds.
For the Black Christian conservative, this personal faith — which is
both heritage and heartfelt conviction — provides strength. It allows
individuals to honor God while also honoring their history and the
community from which they spring. This chapter aims, firstly, to
illustrate precisely how one can uphold their Jesus-over-Black identity without capitulating to dominating ideologies, even when those
ideologies appear to be the voice of a collective culture.

Authenticity is the gold standard against which all else is measured
— it requires no masks and no pretense. For the believer, the authenticity of one's spiritual life is as critical as breath. This quest for genuine
self-expression within one's community without compromising one's
core values sits at the heart of this exploration. Here, readers will learn

the dance of maintaining authenticity while valuing the community bond. This balance is the essence of true belonging — where individual principles are respected within the wider spectrum of communal existence.

Throughout this book, the themes of conflict, identity, and integration have been interwoven like strands of a tapestry. Here, in the penultimate chapter, they converge, compelling readers to step into the fullness of their transformed identity. The Black Christian conservative stands at the crossroads of cultural allegiance and biblical fidelity. By embracing a Christian and conservative identity, they find peace in reconciling faith with social ideologies, and they achieve this without succumbing to the pressure of conforming to mainstream beliefs.

Crafting Identity Through Faithful Endurance

Ultimately, this navigational process is not a solitary experience. It is etched in daily interactions with family, within the bustling activity of marketplaces, and the silent reflection within church walls. This book humbly seeks to serve as a mentor, a guiding voice amidst the noise — a voice that whispers, "Stay the course, uphold your values, and while it may be arduous, the rewards of an integrated life are profound and lasting."

The solutions presented in the preceding chapters build towards this, the chapter that ties it all together. By elucidating with clarity and reverence, the text has paved the way for readers to step into their own stories with a renewed sense of purpose and possibility. What emerges is an affirming echo of a shared experience, one that resonates deeply within the Black Christian conservative's journey.

The messages contained here are more than philosophical pondering; they are a loud call to action. They invite readers to take a stand, to be the venerable oak in a forest wavering in the winds of change, to lead by example, and to be the change they want to see in their communities. This chapter closes the circle, not as an end but as a continuation — prompting readers toward a future defined by harmony between heritage and heartfelt convictions, a future where faith is indeed anchored, and community warmly embraced.

Living in a world where ideologies seem to constantly clash, it can be a profound challenge to remain steadfast in our faith-based conservative values. Yet, it is entirely feasible to stay true to these principles without succumbing to the sway of dominant societal beliefs. The key lies in understanding and articulating the foundations of our convictions and recognizing the intrinsic strength and validity that they hold. Grounded in spiritual teachings, our moral compass should not waiver with the prevailing winds of opinion, but should be the anchor that holds firm in all tides of societal discourse.

One potent way to honor our Jesus-first identity is by actively engaging in conversations with both openness and assertiveness. We must be comfortable in discussing our viewpoints, doing so with both grace and conviction. While we invite dialogue and respect differing perspectives, it is crucial that we do not compromise on the core tenets of our faith. At the same time, we must guard against the tendency to isolate ourselves; the intent isn't to insulate but to inform and be informed, enabling a mutual understanding where possible.

Maintaining authenticity in our beliefs also involves a degree of vulnerability — admitting that having conservative values doesn't necessarily provide all the answers to life's complex questions. It requires us to listen, learn, and sometimes incorporate new insights into our worldview without losing sight of our spiritual and moral foundations. By doing so, we not only strengthen our own convictions, but we also build bridges with those who might initially appear to be on the opposite side of the ideological spectrum. When we need more answers, we can always come back to God and to His Word.

Moreover, it is through the demonstration of our convictions in our professional and personal lives that we can truly validate them. Let your actions speak the language of your beliefs — be it through charity, community service, or the kind of leadership you exhibit. Actions often speak louder than words, and a life lived in harmony with one's beliefs is the most persuasive testimony one can give.

However, we must beware of becoming dogmatic. It is equally important to approach our convictions with humility and a willingness to be wrong. There is wisdom in acknowledging the limits of our understanding and being open to growth. A reasoned position tempered with humility can overcome many barriers and extend the reach of conservative Christian ideologies in a meaningful and respectful manner.

It begins with self-awareness, understanding that to be true to oneself does not mandate the alienation of others. The core of Christian teachings emphasizes love and respect for God and for one's neighbors, even in the midst of profound disagreements. By grounding oneself in spiritual wisdom, it is possible to maintain convictions without being confrontational, thus preserving the fellowship. Remember the Apostle Paul's advice in Romans 12:18, *"If it is possible, as far as it depends on you, live at peace with everyone."* This principle, when lived out, becomes a beacon guiding interactions with the community.

Embarking on this path means recognizing that authenticity and community are not mutually exclusive. One can stand firmly within their conservative values, while also contributing to the community's well-being and progress. For instance, focus on shared goals that align with conservative principles, such as the importance of family, the value of hard work, and the strength that comes from unity. By engaging in conversations and initiatives around these common ideals, one affirms their identity while fostering community solidarity.

Leadership in a community setting often necessitates making tough decisions. As a faith-based conservative, you might find yourself in situations where your principles are tested. In such moments, recall Joshua 1:9 for encouragement, *"Be strong and courageous."* Have the wisdom to navigate complex issues while being transparent about your stance. Authentic leadership draws respect, even from those who might disagree with you, and offers a model of conviction that can inspire others.

Setting boundaries is also a part of maintaining authenticity. It is crucial to discern which compromises are acceptable and which are not. This process is not about isolation but about ensuring you do not lose sight of who you are. By exercising this discernment, based on the teachings of Christ and the wisdom of Scripture, you demonstrate a resolve that contributes positively to both your sense of self and the community's rich tapestry.

In the professional sphere, authenticity might translate to making bold business choices that reflect one's values. It may involve ethical practices that prioritize people over profit or investing in community advancement. Whatever the case, these actions communicate a powerful message: one can be both a person of faith and an innovative leader. The business world, often seen as a playing field for cutthroat competition, can also be an avenue for compassionate capitalism.

Participating in the community does not mean surrendering one's beliefs; it's about engaging with respect and compassion. This engagement is an ongoing process, where learning and teaching go hand in hand. Share your journey and listen to the stories of others. Through this mutual exchange, common ground can be found, and relationships can be built that transcend ideological divides.

Social cohesion and difference of opinion can coexist in the same space if approached with maturity and understanding. Embrace your Christian conservative ethos, using it as a compass for action rather than a barrier to connection. By presenting your truths with confidence and humility, you offer a unique perspective that can enrich the collective conversation. In turn, the community becomes strengthened not in spite of its diversity, but because of it.

Thus, the dance between heritage and heart involves a strategic interweaving of self-knowledge, principle, and participation. It's about being an active member of the community while honoring the inner compass of your faith, aware that it is neither compromise nor conflict but coexistence that molds a harmonious society. **Remember that your convictions do not overshadow the vast expanse of common ground available for unity and cooperation**. In navigating these shared spaces with wisdom and authenticity, the harmony between individual identity and community belonging is not just a goal — it is a vibrant reality.

Defining Your Core Convictions

Consistency in identity begins by defining your core convictions. This is an active process, akin to constructing the blueprint for a building that will weather both sunshine and storms. **Take time to discern the non-negotiables of your faith, those principles that guide your daily decisions and long-term aspirations. How do these convictions align with or differ from your cultural heritage?**

Exploring these questions fosters a grounded sense of self that can navigate the complexities of varied societal expectations.

Fostering Authentic Relationships

Human connection is fundamental as part of God's original design in creation, and pursuing a path of faith-based conservatism doesn't mean isolating yourself from those who think, believe, or vote differently. On the contrary, crafting an authentic identity involves fostering relationships with both like-minded individuals and those outside your circle. This enriches your perspective and reinforces the notion that respect and understanding are cornerstones of genuine community belonging.

Embracing Courageous Conversations

One of the hallmarks of a coherent identity is the courage to engage in difficult conversations. Whether discussing politics, economics, or differing theological views, approaching dialogues with both conviction and compassion is crucial. It's not about winning debates but about respecting others' perspectives while clearly articulating your own stance, thereby fostering an environment of mutual learning and growth.

Balancing Tradition with Innovation

A harmonious blend of faith and heritage also involves recognizing the value in tradition while being open to innovation. Respecting the past does not preclude us from contributing to the future. Entrepreneurs and business professionals can serve as catalysts for positive change within their communities, harnessing the power of their convictions to create solutions that honor their heritage while pushing the boundaries of what's possible.

Living Out Your Faith in the Public Square

For those who aspire to leadership, living out your faith in the public square with integrity is an act of both service and witness. It's about embodying the principles you stand for, whether in public policy, social activism, or community service. This approach not only upholds your beliefs but also demonstrates to others the transformative impact of a life led by faith-based values.

Cultivating Personal and Professional Growth

Remember that **personal and professional growth** are intertwined with your journey. Immerse yourself in continuous learning, whether from theological, political, or economic perspectives, to strengthen your understanding and approach to the world. By doing so, you position yourself to make well-informed decisions that are reflective of both your faith-defined worldview and your cultural heritage.

Navigating with Wisdom and Discernment

In summary, thriving with a coherent identity at the confluence of faith and cultural heritage requires wisdom and discernment. It's about understanding the times, knowing when to stand firm and when to seek common ground. Stepping into the fullness of your beliefs with confidence allows you to navigate the diverse landscapes of your personal and professional life with poise and purpose. Remember, your journey is one of unity—melding the timeless truths of your faith with the richness of your cultural narrative to live a life of impactful authenticity.

Honor and Identity: The Final Synthesis

As we stand at the culmination of this journey, it is paramount to recognize that honoring our faith-based conservative identity in an era swarming with dominant liberal ideologies is not just attainable, but it is a testament to the strength and richness of our cultural and spiritual heritage. Authenticity must prevail as we tread the path that aligns with our heartfelt convictions. We have unraveled the tapestry of pressures and expectations, yet emerged with a coherent identity that unites the fiber of our faith with the colors of our African-American lineage.

Navigating these realms, this book has illuminated the pathway for all of us seeking to reconcile our Christian faith with the currents of social and political life. The strategies and principles expounded here are not mere theoretical concepts, but real-world tried-and-tested methodologies fostered through the experiences and wisdom of those who paved the way before us.

The Pathway Forward

In navigating our rich and diverse identities, our conviction has been our north star—guiding us to navigate the complex waters of modern ideology without surrendering the true essence of who we are. Each chapter has progressively built a robust framework, empowering you, the reader, to undertake this transformational ascent to a life harmonizing spiritual faith and conservative principles.

This journey, while challenging, has revealed that within our steadfastness lies boundless potential. The transformation of your identity that prioritizes Jesus over your race is both a personal triumph and a beacon of hope for others wrestling with similar struggles. The essence of this transformation is not one of seclusion but of inclusion without ideological erosion.

May the insights and narratives from various disciplines—be it theology, politics, or economics—be the compass that helps you to remain rooted in your convictions. As we draw this dialogue to a close, remember that the world benefits tremendously from the breadth and depth of your contribution, glowing with the harmony of shared heritage and strong convictions, magnified by the chorus of the community, and emboldened by the unstoppable force of faith.

A Journey Concluded, A Pathway Unveiled

As we close this chapter of discovery and empowerment, it stands clear that the walk of a Black Christian conservative is not a solitary journey, but one marked by the echoes of those who tread before us, fueled by the courage of their convictions and the unwavering anchor of their faith. Through these pages, we have embarked on a pilgrimage towards reconciling our spiritual beliefs with our political ideologies, unearthing a harmonious existence that neither compromises faith nor stifles the voice of conservatism within our vibrant community.

The Gospel has always been about transformation - the renewal of the mind and the refreshing of the spirit. In your hands, you hold not just a book, but a compass for navigating the complexities of modern societal narratives with your faith in Jesus as your northern star. By intertwining scriptural teachings and conservative principles, a blueprint for living authentically emerges, one that honors both your heritage and your Heavenly Father.

This journey has fostered an understanding that black conservatism is not an anomaly, but a testament to the nuanced tapestry of black thought and identity. It equips believers with the resolve to stand firm in the face of cultural and political adversities, fortified by the strength of communal faith and the conviction of personal belief systems.

The teachings here serve not as an end, but as a beginning – the starting point for integrating a conservative Christian ethos into every facet of your existence. Reflect upon the keystones that have underscored our discussions: the sacredness of life, the pursuit of justice, the reverence for family, and the stewardship of resources. These are not merely intellectual concepts but living, breathing doctrines that animate our steps. Embrace these truths as both shield and sword in the pursuit of a life that is pleasing to God and edifying to the world around us.

Forward Steps

There is more to explore, more to question, and more uncharted waters to navigate. It is both a privilege and a responsibility to forge ahead, guided by the Holy Spirit and equipped with the knowledge invested within you.

Emboldened by the sacred texts and teachings that have illuminated this path, I beckon you to venture forth, not as passive recipients of wisdom but as active participants in the dialogue that shapes our society. Let the lessons here spark conversations, inspire service, and instill a confidence that shines as a beacon of righteous conservatism.

A Call to Embrace Your Identity

Take pride in the duality of your heritage – as children of the Most High God and as stewards of a shared Black cultural heritage and history. Let this book be the anchor that cements your faith, even as you build bridges within the community that lauds diversity yet often shuns the conservative voice within it. Stand as exemplars of a faith that is unfettered by societal labels, and as a testimony to the transformative power of living a life anchored in Christ and the Word of God.

May you go forth with the knowledge that this is not the end, but a reaffirmation of the journey ahead. Carry this message of faith anchored conservatism in your heart, as armor against the forces that seek to disassemble your identity, as comfort in times of doubt, and as inspiration for fellow believers yearning for their own reconciliations.

Parting Wisdom

"Never be limited by other people's limited imaginations."
   – Dr. Mae Jemison
   This profound sentiment encapsulates our call to rise above the constraints placed upon us, to live in the fullness of the identities that God has fashioned for each of us. As we part, let this truth guide you onward, proving that a voice that chooses Jesus over one's race is not simply a whisper in the darkness, but a resounding chorus of diversity, strength, and unwavering conviction.

ABOUT THE AUTHOR

W hat is most important to Philip Blackett and what truly forms his identity is his relationship with his Lord and Savior Jesus Christ. Philip's mission for the rest of his life is to Grow God's People, Grow God's Businesses, and Grow God's Kingdom as a good and faithful steward of all God has entrusted him, while having a positive influence on all who he encounters each day as a Kingdom Man.

Professionally speaking, Philip is passionate about helping entrepreneurs and small business owners grow their dream businesses, while utilizing his skillset in sales, marketing and business development. Previously, Philip served as President of Cemetery Services, Inc., a seven-figure business he bought based in the Greater Boston area. It was "his pleasure" to also serve as a Manager for a Chick-Fil-A restaurant.

At FedEx, Philip previously provided support to several senior Marketing executives (including the current CEO) as a Senior Communications Specialist after working on its Corporate Social Responsibility team. Before FedEx, Philip advised investors on Wall Street in New York City as an Equity Research Analyst for Goldman Sachs, where he helped recommend investments in over 100 publicly traded companies across ten industries.

Regarding his education, Philip graduated from the Southern Baptist Theological Seminary with his Masters of Divinity (M.Div) degree with a concentration in Great Commission Studies. He also earned his MBA from Harvard Business School. In college, Philip graduated from the University of North Carolina at Chapel Hill as a Morehead-Cain Scholar, majoring in Political Science and Economics.

Philip is a Life Member of Alpha Phi Alpha Fraternity, Inc. When he is not actively fulfilling his mission, Philip enjoys reading, watching sports, and raising his twin daughters, Sofia and Elizabeth, with his wife Mayra.

BOOKS BY PHILIP

Disagree without Disrespect: How to Respectfully Debate with Those who Think, Believe and Vote Differently than You

Future-Proof: How to Adopt and Master Artificial Intelligence (A.I.) to Secure Your Job and Career

The Unfair Advantage: How Small Business Owners can Use Artificial Intelligence (A.I.) to Boost Sales, Outsmart the Competition and Grow their Dream Businesses without Breaking the Bank

Jesus over Black: How My Faith Transformed Me into a Conservative within the Black Community

Maverick Lineage: What I Learned about Black Conservatism in America

Bridging the GOP Gap: How the Republican Party can Win Over African American Voters with Inclusivity and Trust without Compromising Values

CONNECT WITH PHILIP

f

facebook.com/PhilipBlackettFB

🐦

twitter.com/PhilipBlackett

in

linkedin.com/in/philipblackett

📷

instagram.com/philipblackett

▶️

youtube.com/@PhilipBlackett

♪

tiktok.com/@pblackett

Facebook:
https://www.facebook.com/PhilipBlackettFB
X (Twitter):
https://twitter.com/PhilipBlackett
LinkedIn:
https://www.linkedin.com/in/philipblackett
Instagram:
https://instagram.com/philipblackett
YouTube:
https://www.youtube.com/@PhilipBlackett
TikTok:
https://www.tiktok.com/@pblackett
Blog:
https://www.PhilipBlackett.com